# Pete Brown
## *The Poet who Rocks*

**Marc Shapiro**

THIS BOOK IS DEDICATED
TO THE LOVE OF MY LIFE
NANCY SHAPIRO
1949-2021

# Pete Brown
## *The Poet who Rocks*

**Marc Shapiro**

WYMER PUBLISHING
Bedford, England

First published in 2023 by Wymer Publishing
Bedford, England www.wymerpublishing.co.uk Tel: 01234 326691
Wymer Publishing is a trading name of Wymer (UK) Ltd

Copyright © 2023 Marc Shapiro / Wymer Publishing.

Print edition: **ISBN: 978-1-915246-25-7**

Edited by Jerry Bloom.

The Author hereby asserts his rights to be identified
as the author of this work in accordance with sections
77 to 78 of the Copyright, Designs & Patents Act 1988.

All rights reserved. No part of this publication may be
reproduced or transmitted in any form or by any means,
electronic or mechanical, including photocopying, or any
information storage and retrieval system, without written
permission from the publisher.

This publication is sold subject to the condition that it shall not,
by way of trade or otherwise, be lent, re-sold, hired out or
otherwise circulated without the publishers' prior consent in any
form of binding or cover other than that in which it is published
and without a similar condition including this condition
being imposed on the subsequent purchaser.

eBook formatting by Coinlea.
Printed and bound in Great Britain by
CMP, Dorset.

A catalogue record for this book is available from the British Library.

Typeset/Design by Andy Bishop / 1016 Sarpsborg
Cover design by 1016 Sarpsborg.

Television on
A white noise parade
Of now interest
Bowl games
A blur of bland
And empty hype
Year end wrap ups
Of all news is bad news
For the world tuning out
Trying to remember the good times
Not finding much of that
Lonely
Numb
Tearful
Memories of when there were two of us
When we would spend the last day of the year
At the track
Blowing some money
Eating unhealthy food
That tasted so great
Before racing home
To watch the ball drop
East coast time
So we could say we made it to midnight
Before falling asleep
In each other's arms

*Marc Shapiro*

# CONTENTS

| | |
|---|---|
| AUTHOR'S NOTES EVEN THE AUTHOR GETS THE BLUES | 9 |
| INTRODUCTION PETE BROWN ENDED UP HERE | 15 |
| PETE BROWN WAR CHILD | 21 |
| A WORKING CLASS JEWISH LAD | 24 |
| YOUNG PETE LOST AND FOUND | 28 |
| PETE'S COUSIN REMEMBERS PETE | 33 |
| BOHEMIAN HALF LIFE | 35 |
| THE BIRTH OF THE SCENE | 40 |
| MAKING MONEY, MAKING HISTORY | 45 |
| BROWN DOES HIS THING | 51 |
| BROWN GETS CREAMED | 55 |
| BROWN ON ALCOHOL, DRUGS AND SEX… CLASS DISMISSED | 68 |
| BROWN GETS BATTERED | 72 |
| THAT'S THE FACTS JACK | 79 |
| PIBLOKTO ANYONE | 85 |
| PIBLOKTO IN DECLINE | 90 |
| PETE THE POET | 93 |
| BRUCE AND BROWN BACK TO WORK | 96 |
| GRAHAM BOND… DEAL WITH IT | 99 |
| BROWN TAKES TIME OFF… NOT | 104 |
| PETE'S PREAMBLE TO DANCING WITH MR. D | 110 |
| DANCING WITH MR. D | 111 |
| PETE CAN SING PETE HATES PUNK | 117 |
| ONCE MORE INTO THE BREECH | 120 |
| THE EIGHTIES… AS IN USELESS | 124 |

| | |
|---|---|
| THINGS GET BETTER | 129 |
| SLOW AND EASY 1985 TO 1990 | 131 |
| IT AIN'T EASY: REFLECTION ON NATHAN AND KITTY | 136 |
| PETE HAS A NINETIES MOVEMENT | 138 |
| HIT THE ROAD PETE | 140 |
| WHAT IF… THAW REVISITED | 144 |
| ONE SATISFIED CAT | 146 |
| WHAT A DRAG | 151 |
| I CAN DO THAT | 154 |
| PETE BROWN'S EXCELLENT MISADVENTURES | 158 |
| ROUGH AND TOUGH | 163 |
| MORE AND MORE OF THE SAME | 166 |
| SIDEMAN FOR HIRE | 171 |
| BROWN WATERS AND IN THE MEANTIME | 175 |
| FRONT TO BACK TO FRONT MARRIAGE, CANCER AND OTHER THINGS | 181 |
| THE RELUCTANT BIOGRAPHER | 187 |
| SMILE FOR THE CAMERA | 189 |
| BROWN LOOKS BACK | 192 |
| PETE MEETS PROCOL | 195 |
| THIS YEAR LOOKS GOOD ON PAPER | 199 |
| THE FUTURE IS IN THE MAIL | 201 |
| *SOURCES* | 205 |
| *ABOUT THE AUTHOR* | 208 |

# AUTHOR'S NOTES
# EVEN THE AUTHOR GETS THE BLUES

Pete Brown. British beat poet. Songwriter. Musician. In tons of groups. Has made a lot of records with a lot of great musicians and, when the fates allow, records with his name front and centre and in the creative driver's seat. Continues to make a lot of records with a lot of musicians, some quite notable in respectable circles. Continues to tour at a time when most of us have shuffled off this mortal coil. Outside of a select group of literary/musical/avant-garde circles, Pete Brown is a literal blip on the screen of popular and pop culture sensibilities.

Looking for a mantra? How does Pete Who? float your boat? While scratching your head, consider this. Pete Brown is a living, breathing anomaly in the poetry/songwriting universe, who has managed to get through quite the life while being alternately acclaimed and doomed to long periods of obscurity. He's had periods of relative affluence punctuated by more frequent fiscal crisis. He's well known in certain circles and less than well known in others.

So why in the midst of the madness in the world today would I write a book on somebody who, while notable in many highbrow circles, is in the true sense invisible? Because I felt it was time to do justice and due diligence to Pete Brown. And perhaps more importantly it was time to get my own mind right.

A lot has happened in the past couple of years.

Personally, and emotionally, it's been chaos. Loss has a tendency to do that to people. But this isn't a pity party so on to the next. My reputation as a writer on the pop culture biography scene is best described as quick and dirty. It's a simple formula, some celebrity gets hot, dies or does something stupid. Then you get the call. Need a book in weeks, months and, yes, sometimes days? I never say no. Most of the books I've done have been of familiar, albeit some only momentary, names and, in all candour, I've done a bang up job of getting things right, enlightening and entertaining. Which is why pros get the big bucks.

Sometimes.

But I have thoughts and ideas, most authors do, about taking the unexpected left turn into something just a bit different on occasion. And over the course of a recent past, those ideas are beginning to take flight. *Beatle Wives: The Women The Men We Loved Fell In Love With* is that Beatle book outlier, a story told entirely from the wives' perspective. *Charles Bukowski: On Film* is a hybrid filmography told, largely, from the perspective of filmmakers who attempted to make cinematic sense of the author's hard life.

And in *Pete Brown: The Poet Who Rocks*, the trifecta is complete.

Telling the complete tale of a truly talented individual who has laboured largely in the shadows, getting it done right and, to a large extent, putting the life and times of a person centre stage that not a lot of people know seemed a noble cause on any number of levels. Plus being a total beat freak, a groupie of the people and the times, made this less of a job and more of a pleasant day in the literary playground.

Pete Brown is best known for writing the lyrics, in tandem with Jack Bruce, of all of the short lived yet utterly influential Cream's best-known songs. Yet even in those career making days, he still laboured largely in shadow. But research quickly provided a discography long on diversity of talent with musicians and bands that stretch around the proverbial block.

And then shortly after beginning research on the project

came the bombshell.

One afternoon I received an unsolicited email from... Pete Brown. Yes, that Pete Brown. A person helping me with early research and a long-time friend of Brown's had, unbeknownst to me, contacted Brown and told him that there was this writer in the states doing a book on him. This rarely happens in unauthorised biography lore, and in all candour, I was expecting the worst.

What I got was that Brown was more than willing to help in any way he could and would be available to answer any questions and to provide contact information to people who might help fill in the blanks. Once I got over the shock and surprise, countless emails and interviews ensued. Brown's only request was that I get his story right.

As it turned out, the history behind *Pete Brown: The Poet Who Rocks* had a bit of a backstory. Brown had been toying with the idea of getting his life and times down for posterity for a number of years and round about 2010, he hooked up with another writer (one Harry Shapiro no relation) and a publisher, *J.R. Books*, that was interested. *J.R. Books* would have one proviso. Rather than an as told to memoir, the publisher insisted that the book be told entirely in Brown's own voice. Brown was a bit hesitant. He was the master poet and songwriter but he was not sure he was up to the task of writing about himself in the first person. But he went ahead and *White Rooms & Imaginary Westerns On The Road With Ginsberg, Writing For Clapton And Cream, An Anarchic Odyssey* was soon a real, live book.

In hindsight, Brown had mixed feelings about *JR Books* and their efforts. A copy of the book, on loan from Brown, contained several hardwritten notes from Brown citing editing errors. The book would do respectable but not spectacular business. Reviews were mixed and favourable. This is where things get a bit stealth.

Sometime after its release, Brown took the rights to the book from the publisher. Nothing specific was forthcoming from Brown or the publisher except that Brown now had the book rights, made small attempts at finding another publisher and then put the book aside amidst a rush of other work and no small amount of management and agent issues that would plague him for years...

Flash forward to 2023. Brown gets wind of my project and rings me up.

Early on in my email and telephone exchanges, I found Brown to be forthright, a realist and downright pragmatic. If there were ground rules, they were slight. I could ask any questions I wanted. He would either answer them with much candour and detail, refer me to his comments in *White Rooms & Imaginary Westerns* when he felt old quotes were preferable to anything he could come up with in 2023. If things got a bit too personal, Brown would either politely refuse to talk about them, offer a few passages that would get the point across or, once again refer to *White Rooms & Imaginary Westerns*. It would be to Brown's credit that almost nothing was off limits.

Pete Brown turned out to be a complex and often contradictory cat. Of course, there was the history, the names, dates and places to connect the dots. But Pete Brown is no prefab, paper-thin pop creation. There is also the character of the man to contemplate. He is a legitimate by-product of life, a time in history when the world was torn asunder and he chose to ride things out his way. Pete Brown has proven a blue-collar worker, a salt of the earth, self-effacing working man with a taut literary mind who, in his own words, "I do not like to waste opportunities," he told the author and is known for willingly taking on any challenge. His willingness to just go for it is mind boggling. The enthusiasm is never ending and overwhelming.

And what writing *Pete Brown: The Poet Who Rocks*

would finally drive home would be a look at somebody who was much deeper than the expected pop culture odyssey. You know, you've read enough of them. The sex, the drugs and the rock and roll, all of which will be reported in abundance. But you will also discover that Pete is much deeper a personage than that. He is also about stuff; relationship stuff, vice stuff, making life work in some semblance of normalcy stuff, an awareness of time, place and history stuff. Pete has, to the world at large, never come across as somebody who is a thoughtful cat. But the reality is normal in a world that is often anything but.

I learned a lot writing *Pete Brown: The Poet Who Rocks*. About the man. About the talent. And what a kick it must have been being in his world and watching him do his thing.

*Marc Shapiro 2023*

Pete Brown - *The Poet who Rocks*

# INTRODUCTION
# PETE BROWN
# ENDED UP HERE

Pure and simple. Cream was the definitive power trio of the sixties. Guitar, bass, drums. Clapton, Bruce, Baker. When they made Cream, they broke the mould. But there was much more to Cream than the blues/heavy rock bash and the bombast and the not too subtle hints of a supergroup in the making. A ghost if you will was lurking in the background of the intense albeit short lived period of Cream mania.

A ghost named Pete Brown.

The de facto fourth member of Cream that nobody ever saw or heard until it counted. Which was in the background of hotel rooms and recording studios, churning out memorable lyrics in a journeyman, workman like manner and facing inevitable deadlines that often-precluded sleep, food and no small amount of creative tension.

This was the time when Pete Brown came to the fore. Because Brown was a poet who had recently turned from a British beat style wordsmith of some note in an exploding British poetry scene to a creative arena in some early music/poetry hybrids that more and more incorporated jazz and other popular forms of the day. Brown knew where he was going and knew that poetry and music were cut from the same cloth.

"I don't usually think of my lyrics as poetry," offered Brown in *The Argonist*. "But having said that, some of my lyrics have more poetic content then others. I came from poetry initially and my earlier lyrics had more residue from that. As I progressed, I found that working in more day to day language suited me.[1]

Even before he became known outside of hip, bohemian

circles, Pete Brown was eminently recognisable as a figure of the times. As described by journalist John Kruth in a preamble to an interview with Brown, in *Please Kill Me Magazine*, "Brown was wild looking, frizzy haired, a cross between Jethro Tull's Ian Anderson and sixties radical Jerry Rubin."[2]

Far from being a clever twist of the creative wrist, Brown's transition from poetry to songwriting in the 1960s was just one of many then current rock stars who would take a flyer at the poetic word during the height of their music careers. This trait was particularly evident during the sixties period when Brown was beginning to find his creative rhythms. David Allen (Soft Machine and Gong), Lou Reed (Velvet Underground), Marc Bolan (T. Rex), Pete Sinfield (King Crimson), Phil Lynott (Thin Lizzy) and Robert Calvert (Hawkwind) were all practitioners to varying degrees of the poetry/musical crossover.

Likewise, Brown would make the decision to meld the two forms. He seemed poised to enter as a songwriter and performer. And for Brown, it would be Cream who would hold the keys to the kingdom. During their short lived and hectic tenure as the true monsters of rock, the band was always in dire need of songs and there never seemed to be a whole lot of time. Bruce was ace when it came to the music. But it would turn out that Brown had the Midas Touch when it came to lyrics.

In short order the Brown/Bruce collaboration would produce a total of nine songs for Cream, the most endearing being 'Sunshine Of Your Love', 'White Room', 'I Feel Free', 'Politician' and 'Deserted Cities Of The Heart'. And just like that, Pete Brown, an energetic, enthusiastic, creative entity constantly on the move in music, poetry, songwriting and, yes, performing, was off to the races.

His good natured, salt of the earth personality and an innate drive to be professional and constantly shifting creative passions have to date, seen him continue to be active well into

2023 and well into his eighties. At a time when even the most prolific creative minds have scaled back, retired or departed for the great rock and roll beyond, Pete Brown is still, quite enthusiastically, going strong.

"It's been a busy year," Brown acknowledged. "As long as we can all stay alive that's the main thing. Late in life positivity is nothing new for Brown. It's always been there. "I'm still here and I still have much to say."

Much to say in many shades of talent and character that this author gleaned during several interviews for this book. During one conversation, there would be the ever-present yowl of a baby in the background, courtesy of family friends who were visiting while on holiday. Brown would acknowledge the baby and then it was back to business. No muss no fuss. Brown as Mr. Easy Going.

On another occasion, the Brown family cat would spend a lot of time scratching on Brown's leg, yelling for food. Good clean family stuff and Brown just went with the flow. But the professional side, the ever-ready time for creative action, was never far from his thoughts. Interviews for this book had to be staggered because Brown was always seemingly in the middle of something.

There was studio time for an upcoming project and a series of performances in Germany to prepare for. That's when the timbre in Brown's voice would noticeably change from easy going, family guy, to a straight to the point, have to get my professional house in order tone. Still good natured but with an edge that said it was time to get ready for the gig.

Finding a different facet to Brown's character was always around an unexpected corner. He was fearless and full of truth when it came to certain subjects that might make others of note a bit uncomfortable and evasive. His personal life was largely an open book. Alcohol was no problem. Drugs were no problem. Women were largely an open book.

Until the moment when the question was broached based on an anecdote from the book *White Rooms & Imaginary Westerns* in which there was a time that he fathered two different children literally back-to-back with two different women. Brown was forthright in acknowledging that story and had long ago indicated that he had a good relationship with a daughter and a near non-existent relationship with his son.

But when the author pushed for greater details, Brown went all noble and, in the Jewish vernacular, morphed into a bonified Mench. Brown told a story but on the condition that it not be used in the book. After hearing the story I agreed with his notion that it could be hurtful to certain parties. In exchange he offered some viable, softer quotes, that would acknowledge his feelings and tell a valid story. Brown wanted to tell the whole story and get it right. But there was a line, not surprisingly, that he refused to cross.

Brown has been consistent in pursuing creative adventure wherever life took him and very rarely has said no to any challenge. And, in a creative sense, his talents have been like Mercury.

Brown has been a jack of all trades, a literal Renaissance man, who over the years, has been up for any creative challenge. songwriting, poetry, performing, screenwriting and producer while continuing to be an unknown quantity in the US except for occasional nods for his Cream contributions. A situation he good naturedly promises to remedy at some point.

He has fronted or performed in numerous progressive rock and jazz ensembles such as Battered Ornaments, The First Real Poetry Band, Piblokto. Brown And Friends and Flying Tigers. He's been a good musical team player on any number of other musicians' albums, as both a songwriter and multi-instrumentalist. Pete Brown rarely says no. And, still going strong at age eighty-two, he has history and a long legacy on his side to prove it.

"I realised a long time ago that you had to keep a lot of balls up in the air in order to keep surviving," said Brown to this author. "If it's something you love doing, why should you stop doing it when you're fifty or sixty? Unless you're going nowhere with it."

As if to prove the point, Brown told the author "If I can survive the next few years, and I do have the odd health issue every now and then, so then who knows. I have a lot of stuff I'm doing. I'm working on a new record, the first since 2014, the *Cream: Acoustic* record on which I am heavily featured and there's a chance of a book of lyrics and a new book of poetry."

As matter of fact and to the point as Brown can be in dealing with the inevitable question of his longevity, he is not above having a good-natured laugh at his own reputation as being older than dirt. "I've always been there but I guess I'm just now getting discovered."

But Brown is aware that when you reach his age, well into the eighties, the spectre of getting old is always around the corner. During the research for this book, Brown recalled in an email report that immortality had stepped up to say hi. "I've just had a lovely dose of the flu after being on the road in Germany. I also had a minor stroke because I overworked but it doesn't seem to have done any obvious damage. Nevertheless, I think it's time to slow down."

On a cheerier note, Brown said that prestigious Sussex University has agreed "to take my archive when I disappear so that all of my work will exist in some sort of perpetuity. Hopefully, immortality beckons. It's an idea that I like."

And for Brown, not unlike his personality, has always had a sense of gallows humour lurking just out of sight as he jokingly proclaimed in a *UYC Experience* podcast episode. "At the end of the day, I'm trying to stay alive long enough to bug a lot of people."[3]

Pete Brown - *The Poet who Rocks*

# PETE BROWN WAR CHILD

There's been a story floating around cyber space for quite some time.

To wit: Pete Brown's parents were named John Roemer and Sarah Cooper and that they were never married. Pete Brown, in an email exchange with the author said bollocks to that.

"That legend about my parents whose first names were Nathan and Kitty, is totally bizarre. They were both first generation Brits. I have photos from my parent's wedding. Plus, my parents were mostly so straight that any impropriety would have been impossible."

Brown, in the same email, did acknowledge that his parent's surnames were actually Labovitch and Koniarski and that their family roots were from Russia, Poland and Lithuania. And that the tenor of the times and the fact that they were Jewish forced a name change to Brown and Cohen. "My father changed his name to Brown when he couldn't get a job as Labovitch because of the prevalent antisemitism of the 1930s. My mother's parents changing their name to Cohen as Koniarski probably seemed too alien to the British."

Brown's mother was five months pregnant when the bombs began to fall at 4:00pm on 7th September 1940.

The Blitz, the massive bombing of London by Germany would last eight months and stretch into May 1941. It is of some historical/ironic significance that the very first bombing run of The Blitz was directed at Surrey, England, that struck what was then known as The Surrey Docks, a direct hit that saw the Docks go up in a massive fireball.[4] But long before the bombings of every city and town in the United Kingdom reached a daily, critical conflagration that would level cities and towns and cause countless deaths and endless destruction.

And for the months away from actually being born, the Brown family was playing hit and run with The Blitz. Brown was initially scheduled to be born in Camberwell House in London when a German bomb literally blew the building to bits. The family then found themselves scheduled for the blessed event in a hospital in Surrey when yet another German missile tore into the hospital, effectively forcing Nathan and Kitty to make another war related change of plans.

It was time for Brown and her husband, with Kitty now five months pregnant, to get out of London. Brown recalled that moment in conversation with the author.

"My parents left London because the house I was about to be born in had received a direct hit from a bomb. They got the message and left the city."

The couple had a sense of what was going on and what was changing in a world that had been plunged into madness led by Adolf Hitler's prophetically named Blitzkrieg (Lightning War) and, more importantly, what it meant to them and their unborn child. Not long after The Blitz began, the couple ran for their lives. But not very far.

The town of Ashtead in the Mole Valley of Surrey, England was long noted as a commuter settlement, a mere 15 miles south of Central London. Nathan and Kitty were survivors in the classic Jewish sense of the word, long on determination and faith and, as Kitty entered the final months of her pregnancy, were determined somehow to make it through those dark days. They eventually found a safe haven in a hospital in Surrey and Peter Ronald Brown came into the world on 25th December 1940. Christmas day.

The impact on the new-born would be two levels of importance and irony, one as a Christmas child, of which there would be plenty and second, Pete Brown would come into the world as a war child, his first wails mixing with the constant bombings of The Blitz as London continued to be torn asunder.

That the conjunction of his birth and the ravages of war were a constant in those early months was not lost on Brown as he recalled of those early years of life in conversation with the author.

"I really did not understand what was going on. As a young child, I was quite impressed by the fireworks display and the explosions in the sky. The Blitz was centred primarily in London and we were outside in the country. Having been forced to leave London after the two hospitals I was supposed to be born in were blown to bits, there had already been a big impact on the family."

"I have one memory of when everyone was asleep in the shelter," remembered Brown. "I managed to climb out on a windowsill and watching all the tracer bullets and searchlights, watching the conflict in the night sky. I was really excited by that."

But Brown would not survive The Blitz in a childlike daze as he remembered when talking to the author.

It would be a moment of trauma for the child, a moment that would have repercussions for Brown for years to come. "When I was three in 1944, a bomb that was meant for London went astray and took out a row of houses right next to ours. We were sheltering under the stairs. Our house was fine but the houses right next to ours were blown to bits, while all the while we had been trapped under the stairs. It would be a very traumatic thing for me, especially years later when I was doing drugs and would have moments of claustrophobia and flashbacks to that moment.

# A WORKING CLASS JEWISH LAD

The chances are that if you threw a rock in any direction in the waning days of the assault on Surrey and the surrounding area, it would most likely strike an Englishman, a Scot or an Irishman, with the odd Russian or Lithuanian thrown in for good measure. If your aim was particularly well directed you might have struck a Jew. Or more specifically a member of Pete Brown's family as he recalled in his 2010 memoir *White Rooms & Imaginary Westerns*.

It was not just Nathan, Kitty and Pete. The Brown family, collectively, were a tight knit clan in their newfound home, consisting of uncles, cousins and all manner of extended family members. And the move to Ashtead was, to a large extent, based on security, family and religious identity, reflected Brown. "The whole clan, my parents, my mother's sisters and their husbands, friends, brothers, uncles. We all moved to *Ashtead*. When we got to *Ashtead*, we were the only Jews for miles. We were the first aliens."

The Brown clan quickly found accommodations, cramped as they were, on one of the many rows of houses that populated much of Ashtead as described by Brown to this author. "We lived in a semi-detached house, one of a group of houses. Ashtead was quite the quiet smallish village."

And a smallish village that, Brown's immediate family aside, was extremely light on Jews. Being a Jew in a largely non-Jewish town was uppermost in the lives of the newly arrived family. Brown recalled in an interview with the author that "I was the only Jewish kid in school and, because of that, I had to fight a lot. I didn't always win but I always gave a good account of myself."

Brown seemed to relish revisiting those times, the good and the bad that had lingered long after the end of World War II.

He was candid with the author in acknowledging that a good part of his early upbringing was surrounded by what he felt was the lingering antisemitism of those post World War II days but that he quite naturally, as most children naturally did in those days, did not pay it a whole lot of mind. "My friendships from a very early age transcended the idea of antisemitism. All my friends were Welsh, Scottish and Russian."

But that did not protect him from the obvious bias levelled against Brown that he received during his early years at Woodfield School and teachers that ran the gamut in Browns' memory. From Miss Paice, a quite fair and encouraging presence, to the presence he considered the absolute worst, one Mrs. Binns. He remembered in a telling conversation with the author, "There was obviously a bit of antisemitism directed at me at school. I had some teachers at the time who were really horrible to me. They would give me a hard time and sometimes the kids would give a hard time. But my family was always there for me." In a way.

While far from considering himself what, in today's vernacular would be considered a latchkey kid, Brown would recall candidly during a phone interview that a by-product of the war had driven his parents to always be at work, in their case running a village shoe store. "Like everybody else at the time, my parents were haunted by the depression after the war. The attitude was that everybody wanted a job for life. The security thing was always on their minds and so they always worked. Between school and them working a lot, I probably didn't see them a hell of a lot during the course of a day."

But their relative absence in the youngster's life would be more than balanced by an assortment of aunts and cousins and other relatives who would be there to guide Brown through an early array of interests and intellectual pursuits.

Of particular importance in Brown's coming of age was his grandfather who would regularly take the boy to the local cinema where he would engage in a literal buffet of movies, with an emphasis on westerns and war movies of the day, such as the John Ford classic *Fort Apache* and the unforgettable, for the impressionable youngster, *They Were Expendable* and *She Wore A Yellow Ribbon*. Brown would often concede that those films and others would register and stimulate his young fantasy life.

"When I was seven, I got very much into westerns," he explained in an interview with the author. "I went through a stage where I wanted to be a member of the US Cavalry. I liked the sense of camaraderie in those movies. I loved John Wayne and his sincerity. I wanted to be that kind of hero."

Over the next few years, Brown's Jewish upbringing proceeded at a snail's pace and, in a subtle way, began the odyssey of the young boy in the direction of the power of the word. "My parents spoke a lot of Yiddish around the house and eventually I was able to learn a bit," he told the author. "The language was always interesting to me. That was the beginning of my fascination with language. I loved the sound of the language and the way the words were put together."

Far less successful was his tentative introduction to Jewish tradition and lore, propagated by Brown's parents who, by the time their son had reached age nine, were attempting a bit of a crash course in their religion, something they had, admittedly, had little of in their own lives. Brown had less than loving memories of Sunday mornings in a Hebrew school class in a makeshift synagogue in the nearby town of Epsom.

The services and approach were noticeably dark and off putting which made Brown feel very alien to the process and surroundings. "The services, especially around the holidays of Yum Kippur and Rosh Hashanah were a foreboding place,"

Brown would recall in the book *White Rooms & Imaginary Westerns*, "and the services made me feel even more alien."

In a sense, the failed religious enlightenment was the beginning of Brown's anti-social behaviour and alternative attitudes. "I remembered not being fond of the conventional and I did not like conventional people," he offered in an interview regarding his past.[5]

By the time Brown reached age eleven, Nathan and Kitty had begun a full court emotional press on their son to conform and, to a large degree, follow in their post war footsteps. "They were expecting my conversion to being a lawyer or an accountant," he reflected in a recent interview with the author. "One thing I was certain of was that I would never sell shoes."

# YOUNG PETE LOST AND FOUND

Pete Brown turned eleven in 1951. When he least expected it, his parents dropped a bit of a bombshell on him.

After an exploratory visit to London and an examination at Hasmonean Grammar School, Nathan and Kitty packed up and moved to London, the better for Pete to experience a traditional Jewish life, unlike their own.

In a wide-ranging interview in 2022, Brown recalled being less than thrilled. "When they decided I needed to be more Jewish and we moved to London, it was a huge change for me and I hated that. All of a sudden I couldn't be with my friends and I could only be around Jewish people. I was very upset by that."

Hasmonian was a school founded on the best of intentions. It's founder, Rabbi Dr. Solomon Schonfield, who was already perceived a hero in Jewish lore for saving the lives of thousands of Jews during the Holocaust, created Hasmonian as an educational and cultural refuge for largely displaced Jews who had found their way to London. The curriculum was straightforward, a solid Orthodox Jewish education coupled with the goal of funnelling its students in the direction of jobs in the white-collar sector of society.

It all sounded good to everybody. Except Brown, who at a very early age, was already anti everything that smacked of tradition. "From the beginning, I was angry about being there," he recalled. "I didn't want to be part of the Jewish community. I was almost as much of an outsider as when I was the only Jew in the village (*Ashtead*)."

Being the anti-Jewish Jew in Hasmonian was only part of the problem. The strident approach to teaching was another, as was dealing with teachers who had emotional issues that were inevitably passed on to their students. "The impact of the Jewish psyche after the war was massive at all levels. Our teachers had been in the armies and the camps. It would take a whole book to describe what that school was like."

But in the 2010 book, *White Rooms & Imaginary Westerns*, Brown would tear into the institution and the instructors with a vengeance. "There were war veterans with shredded nerves, demented Rabbis and Blitz victims whose hands shook."[6]

Hasmonian was a dire, unpleasant place to be and from that first day in class when he was beaten up by the son of the school principal, Brown related in *White Rooms & Imaginary Westerns*, that he found himself quite at odds with the institution and with good reason. "At that point I was a fully-fledged anarchist in so many ways. In so many ways I hated authority. There were a few of us at that school that kind of gravitated toward each other. We were the outsiders."[7]

Through the first two years at Hasmonian, Brown adopted a go with the flow to get along attitude, essentially playing a game that would make his parents happy. Brown recalled in a *White Rooms & Imaginary Westerns* recollection that "he learned classical Hebrew, prayed two or three times a day and made my parents happy that I was more Jewish than they were."[8]

All of which resulted in Brown having to commit to that time honoured Jewish tradition of becoming a man at age 13 with a *Bar Mitzvah* ceremony. He would remember the moment like it was yesterday in his 2010 book. "I was not a traditional Jew at all and going through the *Bar Mitzvah* was a real chore. For me, it was like doing a bad deed. But I learned my *Torah* and I did it. My *Bar Mitzvah* would be my last real act as part of the Jewish community."[9]

Years later, Brown would often contemplate his antagonistic attitude toward Judaism in particular and religion in general as he thoughtfully contemplated in an interview with *Strange Brew.com*. "I hate religion deeply. I'm afraid that it causes an awful lot of trouble in the world."[10]

But while his ties to the Jewish faith were rapidly shrinking, during his third and fourth years at Hasmonian it would be a time when Brown was suddenly expanding his creative horizons.

He had an aunt who, in a literary sense, always had his back as he slowly but surely ventured out into the brave new world of literature and poetry. And while he continued to cling to the fascination of westerns and war, imagery that included an attraction to the classic movie soundtracks, that would stick with him throughout his life, those in his circle of outsider friends were slowly but surely showing him the way to a more expansive world.

Victor Schoenfield, Sidney Manken, Geoff White, Lawrence Rogoff and Dan Gillon were Brown's de facto alternative lifestyle educators; teaching him the wonders of bohemianism, jazz and poetry under the always available mantra of 'Hey Pete! Take a look at this! Listen to this."

Brown remembered this alternative education well in conversation with *Please Kill Me*.com. "I started off reading Dylan Thomas and Gerard Manley Hopkins and, through friends of mine, I discovered Frederico Garcia Lorca, Kenneth Patchen and Robert Creeley. Thomas was a big attraction for me because he was anarchic and I was very much that way. At that point, poetry for me was largely word of mouth, things my friends would suggest I read."[11]

Brown would acknowledge in conversation with the author that his early attraction to the Beats came courtesy of the very hip friends he was hanging out with. "It was through a couple of my friends that I got into Ferlinghetti, Ginsberg, Kerouac and the like. The first Beat book I ever read was *Gasoline* by Gregory Corso. The whole Beat thing was something that immediately interested me.

Brown's coming of age musically during this period went hand in hand with the growing presence of jazz and bebop on the London music scene. His first experience seeing a live jazz band was at The 45 Jazz Club just around the corner from where he lived. He recalled from an *All About Jazz.com* excerpt from the book *White Rooms & Imaginary Westerns* that his early attraction to the world of jazz records was anything but predictable. "I was always fairly eclectic in the early records that I bought. The first two records that I bought were by Stanley Bechet and Gerry Mulligan. Then I was into the twenties for a while, things like King Oliver and then I was into early Duke Ellington."[12]

By his fourth year at Hasmonian, Brown had essentially left the concept of a formal Jewish life and education behind as he was out and about experiencing poetry and jazz that fired up his imagination as he told this author. "My imagination would just take off. When I was supposed to be doing schoolwork, I would just be off doing my own thing." Brown would put an emphatic and poetic exclamation point on his break with tradition when he offered in *White Rooms & Imaginary Westerns* that "The bohemian life had me by the scruff of the neck and there seemed no going back."

The urge to do something truly creative with his life seemed to be everywhere he turned. He recalled in a *Songs Mean Something* interview that "Hearing a recording by poet Kenneth Patchen was a seminal experience for me as it opened some thought of avenues of poetry and music."

But Brown's first real push into actively pursuing creative efforts on a personal level came from a truly unexpected source — his *English* teacher Dr. Levine — who sensed that Brown's anti authority attitude was concealing creative frustrations trying to get out. "Dr. Levine approached me one day and said 'Look. The kinds of things you're putting into your essays are the kinds of things I think you should be doing on your own'."

Brown began his first attempts at writing poetry. By his own estimation, those early poems were very much an imitation of what Dylan Thomas wrote. And Brown, in all candour, felt that those first poems were not very good. But Brown had found an outlet for a lot of his attitudes, eventually developing a writing style that was his.

Much of his fourth year at Hasmonian would be a blur. He would literally sleepwalk through his classes, not showing much enthusiasm for his Jewish education while spending a lot of time with his bohemian circle, taking short road trips, hanging out listening to jazz and fuelling an anti-establishment attitude that had by this time reached critical mass with both Brown and the school. Theological disagreements and a series of suspensions (as diplomatically chronicled by *Culture Court. Com*) had become common but the proverbial last straw for all concerned would be at the end of the year final exams, being very much undiplomatic, Brown recalled the day of the school's all important religious exams and how, as reported in *White Rooms & Imaginary Westerns,* his group responded.

"The ungodly among us revolted," said Brown in the book. "Some turned in blank papers. I went much further and decorated mine with bugs, knives and airplanes. I got thrown out of the room and put outside the headmaster's room for being cheeky. The headmaster found me, realised what had happened and expelled me on the spot. I was now in limbo."[13]

# PETE'S COUSIN REMEMBERS PETE

Brown's Cousin Elaine Grazen was five years older than him and admits in conversation with the author that there was a lot about the young boy in the early, formative days that escaped her. But she recalled the small moments, the days when young Pete would take her brother hunting for newts, the closeknit nature of the Brown family and, perhaps more insightful, his coming of age as a creative being and his parents' less than thrilling response to his unorthodox aspirations during email interview.[14]

"I saw more of Pete when his parents moved to Hendon Way. He was often in and out of our house. He was very close to my parents who were not from the business world, who were the first in all of our families to go to university and were very much non-judgmental. Even at a very early age he was more interesting and glamorous than any of my other cousins. He particularly liked to talk to my mother who had the distinction of being the first Jewish editor of *The Catholic Herald*. Around the time he started getting into writing he would often come over and talk to my mother about what he was writing and what he was doing creatively."

As the years went by and the young boy got deeper into poetry and the early stages of the bohemian lifestyle, Grazen had a front row seat at the growing divide between Brown and his tradition bound parents. "Pete's parents did not get it (his fascination with writing and poetry) and I think they made it very clear to him. I suspect the other aunts and uncles were equally dismissive of him. And in a way their reaction was not surprising. The second generation of immigrant families had to work very hard to make a living and would have found anything in the arts to be indulgent. I think Pete's parents wanted him to have a conventionally secure future. I would imagine his parents were chronically disappointed by Pete."

But Grazen's family would remain steadfast in their support of Brown as he grew into some notoriety, always attending his poetry performances when they could, attempting, on some level, to show him the support he was not getting from his parents. However Grazen steadfastly acknowledged that Brown remained totally committed to his parents and, even as his stature in the literary world grew, he would always make time to visit and be with his parents.

"There was never any doubt that Pete loved his parents and was loyal to them. No matter how different they were."[15]

# BOHEMIAN HALF LIFE

Limbo would not set well with Brown's parents. Nathan and Kitty had long been vocal, predicting dire life consequences for their son who, even at a young age, was chaffing against traditional values. But while they would spend much of the ensuing summer unsuccessfully attempting to get their son reinstated at Hasmonian, for his part, Brown, by now fully caught up in his passions, was having none of it during the summer of 1956.

"My parents went to the headmaster and begged him to take me back," Brown reflected in an interview with the author. But at that point, the only thing I was interested in was jazz. I was obsessed with jazz. I did nothing but go to jazz clubs and listen to jazz."

But there was more to Brown absorbing the bohemian life than the music. The young man had devoured the vibe of Kerouac and *On The Road* and when, along with a school chum, the opportunity presented itself to hit the road, Brown jumped at the chance. In the course of two weeks, Brown and his buddy hitchhiked at leisure up the country to Scotland, staying in youth hostels, occasionally in tents and meeting all sorts of interesting people along the way. Brown still remains enthusiastic years later in conversation with the author. "It was great. I loved it. It was the first time I had really been out on my own in the world. It was a good time in my life to be out and about "

But Brown also recalled that upon returning home, he was once again on the receiving end of his parent's pressure to drop the fantasy notions and to conform. He would lay up in his room for hours and days, listening to jazz while his parents nattered at him from all sides. "My parents finally told me 'well if you're not going back to school, then you're going to have to get a job.' So I went and got a job."

The Heather Garage was not the type of employment option Nathan and Kitty would have hoped for their son. Located down a side street in a seedy section of London's Jewish community, The Heather Garage was a no frills, greasy, dirty lower-class establishment populated by working-class non-Jewish mechanics. For Brown, the experience would be a double-edged adventure. He would learn the basics of car maintenance and would become quite good at tyre repairs. But the downside would be that he was, the only Jew in the shop, constantly bombarded with anti-Jewish comments and putdowns. "I would always hear things like 'What's a fucking Yid like you doing working here?' I was always hearing about how the Jews were taking the jobs away from working class Gentiles."

Brown would prove quite good at the mechanic trade and his parents could not argue with the fact that he was bringing home a reasonable working man's wage. But Nathan and Kitty, still set in their traditionalist ways, also felt that their son was bringing a sense of shame to the family name and began looking around for a way for their son to step out of the grease pit. It was then that they discovered that The Regent Street Polytechnic School Of Modern Languages offered a one year course in journalism that, they felt might be more attuned to their son's more creative tendencies. It also did not hurt that the course was offered free.

Nathan and Kitty approached their son with this option to staying on at the garage and would, by association, allow them to hold their heads a little higher at family gatherings. Brown would have another reason to agreeing to try it. "Journalism school was just a year's course and I was tired of being a labourer,"

Brown's agreement to attempt employment as a member of the fifth estate went a lot further than escaping the clutches of a blue collar, working stiff life. He was amused at the prospect of being a journalist but was essentially in it to keep his parents off his back for a while and to use journalism school as a smokescreen to further advance his bohemian lifestyle. The school, which Brown would describe as "The Big Lie Factory" in *White Rooms & Imaginary Westerns* was on a par with his time at Hasmonian as the instructors seemed, to Brown, more interested in turning out by the numbers hacks than anything approaching a legitimate creative path.

Brown would concede that, from a purely practical view of the school's stated goals, his time in Regent was not a total waste of time as he would acknowledge in *The Head And Heart.com* interview. "I was there for nine months. I did not graduate but I did learn some technical things along the way that I think helped me out. I know during that time I started to think that I might just be able to make a living doing what I wanted to do."[16]

There would be one important historical note attached to Brown's brief tenure at Regent Street Polytechnic. He was continuing to write poetry, still much in the vein of Dylan Thomas/Gerald Manley Hopkins, and while not totally satisfied with the efforts, his first official poetry publication would be in the school's literary magazine *Slant*. The publication in *Slant* was a small victory but an encouraging one. While he would continue to essentially go through the motions in journalism school, Brown's drive to become part of bohemian society was uppermost.

Brown's appearance in *Slant* quite literally had the youngster on cloud nine," he recalled in conversation with the author. "I loved it. What I was writing at the time was not great stuff but the poetry thing was good at the time because I was giving birth to something that was creative. Of course it looked terrible to my parents. They were terrified at the politics of what I had written."

What is known of that period is that Brown was very much about hanging out with hip friends, attending parties, chasing after women in an often-comical attempt to lose his virginity, the first uneasy attempts at mastering the likes of the trumpet in the *Regent* rehearsal band and sandwiching in mundane and dispiriting dead end jobs.

By 1958, Brown was essentially running a con on his parents and, perhaps, himself, doing just enough conservative things to keep them off his back while taking every opportunity to have a creative life. "I was quickly removing myself from their sphere of influence," he recalled. "I was living a strangely mixed-up life."[17]

Brown was officially out of journalism school and out on his own. But being a budding poet/bohemian was not paying the bills and it was not long before he found himself dragged back into the casual labour pool, doing such mundane dirty work as cleaning toilets in restaurants and selling programs at sporting events.

But for Brown, living a lie in his own head would eventually reach a breaking point while working the latest in a long line of low paying jobs as a clerk in a textile warehouse. "There was this nonentity of a clerk who I sometimes spoke to," Brown related in his autobiography. "He came in one morning, hung up his hat and coat and dropped dead. I took this as a sign. I allowed myself to be fired. It was my last regular London job."[18]

The period 1958-1960 found Brown quite literally on his own, travelling the roads throughout the UK, experiencing the fragments of early jazz and poetry scenes, continuing to evolve as a fully formed man of words and, as he recalled, giving what would be his first live poetry readings during one of his many excursions to Scotland. "I went to Scotland and, in exchange for room and board, I would give private poetry readings. These would be my first poetry readings, except for the occasions when I was trying to impress girls. I liked it. I felt comfortable performing."

It would be during the late fifties that Brown, poetically speaking, would dent the poetry ceiling when one of his poems would appear in the very important for its time US literary magazine *Evergreen Review*. In fact, Brown's debut appearance in *Evergreen Review* would be two poems, *Africa and Small Poem* (Issue No. 10 December/January 1959). Brown laughingly recalled in *MusicGuy247.com* that *Small Poem* was literally that. "The poem read/ I write a poem/I threw it in the river/The fish thought it was bread/And they ate it." Brown would subsequently make a second appearance in *Evergreen Review* (Issue No. 18 May/June 1961) with the poem *Thoughtful*.

Brown would assess his *Evergreen Review* successes as part and parcel of his continued growth as a poet as he related in *Music From The Head And Heart.com*. "I wrote a couple of sonnets just to see if I had the chops. I felt rather excited with that. I was still a bit of an outsider so those poems gave me a raison de'tre."[19]

All self-effacing aside, the reality was that Brown was now a published poet in the *Evergreen Review*. The poems were short and, by degrees, primitive but to the reading public it was a pretty big deal.

Pete Brown was officially on the map.

# THE BIRTH OF THE SCENE

By 1960, Brown and his parents were essentially on the outs with each other and, to a large degree, he blamed himself. "A lot of the bad feeling was my fault for being impossible. But their wilful incomprehension didn't help. They had a hostile attitude toward my friends who they blamed, with some justification, for me being how I was."[20]

And so Brown was on his own and into a full blown lifestyle of jazz, poetry, art, drink and continued failed attempts with women. Brown was still a rank amateur in the poetry world, occasionally performing at little out of the way dives and cellars. But the timing could not have been better because the influence of the US Beats across the pond and the onset of pop music as something more than noise and puppy love was on the march.

Brown would acknowledge in a conversation with *All About Jazz.com* that, by 1960, a creative line was definitely being crossed. "For a long time, the poetry scene had been dominated by posh voices and academics. I would hitchhike around Britain giving readings and it was such a rich place regionally and vocally. There was the influence of the Beats and all these poets who were coming forward with strong regional voices which I thought was fucking wonderful. We were breaking down the wall with real voices."[21]

John Mumford, a young trumpet player who sensed that the accepted forms of bebop were exploding along with the more adventuresome sounds of Charlie Mingus and Miles Davis, was one of those who saw something new on the horizon. In an interview with this author, Mumford acknowledged that the UK scene was being bombarded with reports of more exciting scenes popping up in places like Greenwich Village and San Francisco and that the desire for something new was filtering down from the poets and jazzers to the public at large.

"The combination of poetry and jazz was very new to the public," recalled Mumford. "British audiences were not used to seeing and hearing something so different. For the longest time they had been used to cautious reviews or cabaret put on by the 'University Circuit'. All of a sudden there was this new, semi anarchic, disrespectful mindset that struck attractive and definite chords with a younger generation who felt the approach of all manner of possibilities."[22]

If this all sounded like a movement in the making, a sudden wave of a new breed of British poets, that besides Brown would include the likes of Adrian Mitchell, Roger McGough and Brian Patten, would seem to over complicate matters. Like all true movements, what was beginning to surface in 1960 British literary circles, was, quite simply, shared creative minds and interests coming together with a keen interest in upsetting traditional, long held values and attitudes. So call it what you will, when Brown was reading his poetry in front of sparse crowds and impromptu settings, there was that sense of discovery and, yes, a sense of revolution in the air.

Brown would concede some years later that those early gigs were conspicuous by audiences that could be counted on two hands and still have some fingers left over. "One of the first things I did was at the outer fringes of the Edinburgh Festival," he said in a *MusicGuy 247* interview. "There was about eight other poets, one girl, one baby and a dog. It was a small scene."[23]

It was a small scene but a pivotal one for Brown and other poets as, at the conclusion of the reading, a hat was passed and the handful of shillings was given to Brown. "I got a few shillings so at that point I was not an amateur anymore," Brown told this author. "It all felt quite natural. I decided at that point that I would try and make a go of this."

Which meant that Brown would continue to live in

squalor, which he explained to journalist Chris Welch in an excerpt from *Encyclopedia.com* "I was busy being a beatnik and living in a slum with a lot of other people."[24]

Poets in the UK underground, much like the lives of pop stars of the day were ripe with possibilities and perks, sex and drugs being the most obvious of those. In a bit of candour, Brown told the author about his descent into both arenas. "I did some drugs and I did drink a lot. For me, it kind of disguised some shortcomings that I had. Because of my insecurities, I was a virgin longer than most of the others. Eventually there were some women who came along and helped me out. By the mid-sixties, I was no longer a virgin."

Brown's earliest travels as a de facto poet would, in 1960, bring him to the Beaulieu Jazz Festival where he would meet Michael Horovitz, an Oxford educated poet of music and letters who was beginning to make waves on the poetry scene with the publication of the literary magazine *New Departures*. Brown would remember that meeting in conversation with *All About Jazz. com*. "It was like Stanley meeting Livingston. We had a lot in common. We both loved jazz and liked a lot of the same writers."[25]

But Brown would concede that, to his way of thinking, it was a cautious courtship. "Mike and I were not instant friends. We were in many ways opposites. Mike had powerful academic credibility and I had none. But we were both Jewish and we both had an ear for language and rhythm."[26]

And as these things often play out, spontaneity among this new wave of wordsmiths and, in particular Brown and Horovitz would pave the way.

A series of intense conversations surrounding the concept of poetry and jazz would erupt out of nowhere and seemingly last forever. Then the pair would go their separate ways for some months, with Brown continuing sporadic hitchhiking adventures and, in December 1960 his first public solo performance. But Brown and Horovitz remained in contact and would do a one-off dual reading at the Edinburgh Festival that primed the creative pump. They sensed that, with *Beatlemania* just around the corner, a new kind of freedom was abroad in normally tradition bound England. They both felt it was time to try something new.

The pair did not have to look far to find musicians up to the new adventure. By this time Mumford had formed a creative alliance with Dick Heckstall-Smith and the pair could regularly be seen jamming at the Café des Artistes and other jazz locals. Mumford's memory was that "At one of those shows, Mike (Horovitz) saw us and contacted us."[27]

"We decided to team up together," recalled Brown in *Please Kill Me.com*. "Mike already had some musicians in tow and wanted to get a regular jazz and poetry group going. It sounded good and so I was in."[28]

Brown and Horovitz decided to give the notion of what their passions of poetry and jazz could be, a practical workout with a series of hybrid performances throughout the remainder of 1960 and sporadically throughout 1961. It was a heady decision. It was a true roll of the dice despite the growing sense that anything in the early sixties was truly possible.

For Brown it would be the best kind of on the job training. Reading poetry with no backing was one thing and, for Brown, had been manageable. Reading his poetry with vigorous musical backings under the banner *Live New Departures Jazz Poetry* was going to be a different animal all together. But the pressure would not be on Brown alone. Mumford was quick to acknowledge that everybody in the band "was both confident and intimidated" at the prospect of stepping into uncharted creative waters.

Festivals in Bangor, Aberystwyth and South Hampton mixed with venues like The Cheltenham Jazz Club and the Oxford Town Hall flew by in a blur of experiences and a growing confidence in both Brown and Horovitz to somehow make a go of all this.

And 'this' would prove to be a true test, a literal avant-garde buffet that, from performance to performance, could be anything at any time as described in *Lux.org.uk* by author Barry Miles. "*Live Departures* was a travelling show with poetry, experimental jazz, fragments of plays, someone painting onstage. It was the introducing of the new avant-garde."[29]

Mumford obviously had an up close and personal take on what *Live New Departures* was doing. "It was not so much a hybrid performance as it was an event. There were no scripts."

*Live New Departures* would also be a lesson for Brown in reading his poetry fronting what was considered top of the line comers in the jazz music scene, a revolving cast, in both a big band and quartet format that, on any given night, would consist of, through Horovitz's contacts, many good jazz musicians of the day that included Stan Tracey, Bobby Wellins, Jeff Clyne, Laurie Morgan, John Mumford and, on occasion, sit ins by the likes of Graham Bond and Dick Heckstall-Smith. Brown, who always had a sense of rhythm and music forms in even his earliest poems, was a quick study to the dynamics of this hybrid form.

Going into 1961, Brown was confident that he was up to the challenge of this creative new world. This was an exciting time. It was time to leave pretence behind. It was time for the poet to turn pro.

# MAKING MONEY, MAKING HISTORY

In all honesty, Pete Brown has always wanted to be famous. And one of the main reasons he wanted to be famous was… Well let Brown explain it.

"The attraction was, as the famous writer who I loved Nathanael West was once asked what made him want to be a famous writer? And he said 'I was hoping that it would make me more attractive to women'" he reflected in *Music From The Head And Heart.com*. "There was that motivation of course. But then there was the fact that it was clear that I wasn't going to fit into any kind of conventional framework of trying to make a living because, quite simply, I was too much of an anarchist."[30]

But while the women were beginning to come Brown's way, the suddenly legitimate (i.e., profitable) rise in poetry and jazz was beginning to get economic traction with the young music centric followers who were always on the lookout for the next hip thing. But Brown did not want to overstate the obvious as explained in *Music Guy 247.com* which was, in the early sixties, thanks to a large extent to Horovitz's connections to slightly more lucrative gigs, everybody was getting paid but not getting rich. "I mean at the best I was earning in American money was about $40 a week or something like that."[31]

When not gigging with *Live New Departures*, Brown would continue his itinerant poet ways, hitchhiking around the UK with little or no money in his pocket in search of a reading and a few shillings. And, more often than not, crossing paths with other poets and musicians who were living the same kind of bohemian life.

Brown would recall in a quote from *Beat Scene Magazine*

that those times were poverty laced but no less stimulating. "We became a loosely knit group, exchanging ideas. The audiences were often small and we created as much for each other as we did for them. We were still very much outsiders, living in varying degrees of squalor. We were very poor but we seemed to drink and get stoned surprisingly often."[32]

Thanks to the largesse of landlords, Brown would often find himself in a communal living condition which, as recalled by musician John Mumford who shared living space with Brown and other poets and musicians, in pre-war lower ground floor apartment on Oppidans Road in Chalk Farm that offered the questionable luxury of a six to a room bunk bed situation, could prove amusing in a surreal sort of way.

"Pete, technically through a loosely interpreted lease situation, was our landlord," related an amused Mumford in conversation with the author. "And because of that he had a more spacious room that gave him the opportunity to occasionally offer space for visitors. There was very little resentment from the rest of us about this. His status as landlord seemed to work pretty well for him. The rest of us were all gratefully aware that he had been cast in a particularly impossible role as the person who had to try and collect the rent money. Pete also had the responsibility for the telephone. When payment demands arrived, we all denied ever using it. There was also an actual kitchen although, at most times, we found it pointless to be in there. Overall, our shared daily income was zero."[33]

*Live New Departures* would slowly but surely make progress. Positive response to their performances and Horovitz's jazz music connections would land the group a 1963 residency at the quickly becoming legendary pit stop for future rock royalty The Marquee Club. It would be a fairly short-lived residency, headlining what were the 'quiet' Tuesday night shows. The group did quite well in The Marquee, the intimate nature of 'quiet Tuesdays' seemed to fit quite well with the group's show.

As fate would have it, busy Thursdays at The Marquee were the residence of, to Brown's way of thinking, the prime blues ensemble, Alexis Korner's Blues Incorporated, which featured a literal who's who on the jazz scene in Dick Heckstall-Smith, Graham Bond, Jack Bruce and Ginger Baker. Because he was allowed into the club for free on nights he was not playing, Brown could usually be found on the nights Korner and company were performing.

Smith and Bond were familiar to Brown because of their occasional sit ins with *Live New Departures* and, through them Brown was introduced to Bruce and Baker. Baker and Bruce had a nodding acquaintance with Brown, having shared the stage at a *Live new Departures* festival.

During early conversations post Marquee Club introduction, Brown recalled that there was an immediate creative connection. "They had both seen me perform live in concert and they knew what I could write," Brown said in *All About Jazz.com*. "They knew that I was very sympathetic toward the kind of music they liked."[34] But it quickly became evident that Bruce and Brown had chemistry. They shared a love of film and jazz and they loved a lot of the same music.

File away for future reference.

If there was a mover and shaker in the mushrooming UK underground poetry scene, well into 1964, the mantle had fallen on Tom Pickard. Pickard, a poet who, with wife Connie, was, much like Brown, very much an advocate of the bohemian lifestyle, and was persistent in living and breathing the emerging UK scene.

On a whim in 1963, the Pickard's decided to open up a bookstore in the long-abandoned remains of a gunnery installation on a west wall in the city of Newcastle. They rented the crumbling remains of *Morden Tower* for a mere ten shillings and soon set upon the arduous and yet spirited task of turning *Morden Tower* into a counterculture bookstore, occasional music venue and a word of mouth gathering place for the young and creatively inclined of the day. Pickard's ambitions for *Morden Tower* included a series of poetry readings by international and British poets.

In an interview with *Poetry Foundation.com*, Pickard recalled the day when, on a hitchhiking odyssey to submit his poetry to a potential publisher, *Scorpion Press*, a stranger stopped and offered him a ride. "I was picked up by a filmmaker named Ian Wood. When we got to talking, I told him about *Morden Tower* and the dreams we held for it. He told me about his neighbour in London, a jazz poet named Pete Brown and suggested that we invite him to do a gig at the Tower."[35]

Brown would jump at the offer. "The poetry thing was very interesting to me at the time," he remembered in *Emptymirrorbooks.com*. Being a young man and very interested in the opposite sex, it was a very good opportunity that I found very gratifying."[36]

Needless to say, Brown readily agreed and, on 16th June 1964, the poet arrived at *Morden Tower* a mere thirty minutes before he was set to perform to an enthusiastic, albeit sparse crowd estimated to be less than thirty people. But Brown recalled in *All About Jazz.com* that it was a good time. "I was the first person to read at the Tower. It was just me reading, no music. It was a terrific place, great atmosphere and the girls were very friendly."[37]

The tide began to turn in 1965. The new wave of British poets and poetry was close on the heels of British rock in terms of popularity and mania. Long story short, poetry was now hip and cool. The venues for people to hear live poetry was growing. More and more poets were starting to make, relatively, more and more money. And across the pond, the poets who had nurtured the British beats were starting to sit up and take notice at what they had inspired.

And now they wanted in on the action.

In May 1965, Ginsberg had come over to London at the request of author/bookstore owner Barry Miles to do a reading at his Better Books store and to get a tour of the London/Liverpool scene. Brown would offer to accompany Ginsberg and, through a series of meetings, parties and eyewitness observations of the flamboyant and spontaneous poet at his often most outlandish.

"I did not know how to react," Brown would recall of those days in his autobiography. "I felt embarrassed. "But I saw Ginsberg as a powerful performer. He was like a very hip rabbi."[38]

In a moment of sheer exuberance during his visit, Ginsberg was heard to exclaim that he would happily do another reading for free. Before the dust had settled on Ginsberg's statement, a loosely based conglomerate of poets, actors and photographers, John 'Hoppy' Hopkins, Dan Richter, Barry Miles and Michael Horovitz had banded together as the International Poetry Incarnation to gather up a vast array of Beat dignitaries and international up and coming poets for a one day event at the Royal Albert Hall on 11th June 1965. The goal was simple, to bring poetry up from the underground and give it a platform to a growing generation of followers.

Given the short prep time, the Albert Hall presentation would be an all-star line-up for the ages.

Allen Ginsberg. Lawrence Ferlinghetti, William S. Burroughs and Gregory Corso were most certainly the frontline attractions. But the event truly did itself proud, introducing the audience to a well-heeled representation of both veterans and young and hungry poets from international corners.

The likes of Pete Brown, John Esam, Harry Fainlight, Pablo Fernandez, Spike Hawkins, Anselm Hollo, Michael Horovitz, Ernst Jandl, Paolo Lionni, Christopher Logue, George MacBeth, Tom McGrath, Adrian Mitchell, Dan Richter, Alexander Trocchi, Simon Vinkenoog and Andrei

Voznesensky gave a constant, riveting object lesson on where the current wave of poets had come from and where it was going. The Albert Hall would sell out in record time, with another 500 being turned away.

*The Incubator.com* was diligent in collecting observations of the poetry blow out. "The poets were not given any running order and the evening ran with very little structure. The audience was given flowers as they entered the arena which, full of a heavy drinking crowd, quickly became filled with marijuana smoke."[39]

Far from being a prude when it comes to drinking and drugs, Brown, who was quite thrilled with the Albert Hall evening, sounded a cautionary assessment of the drinking and drug use that, for many in the audience, enhanced the reading. "The Albert Hall was the start of the acid culture in Britain," he critiqued in *White Rooms & Imaginary Westerns*. "Relatively few people took it although there were a lot more who thought they had. For me, the drug promotion was the downside. It side-lined the feeling that a new ethical consciousness was dawning. Drugs made people selfish and stupid. There was a built-in contradiction. But it was great to see so many spectators at the poetry zoo though and the reverberations were considerable. There was some good art actually escaping from the cage."[40]

But, in hindsight, Brown was never far from the reality that poetry was his way to pay the rent and in looking back on the impact Albert Hall readings had on the emerging scene, his sense of economics as it pertained to the event was never far from his mind. "The whole thing came about because of Alexander Trocchi and all these peripheral figures like Dan Richter and John Esam," he told *All About Jazz.com*. "Somebody ran away with all the money. I don't think any of us ever got paid."

"It was insanity."[41]

# BROWN DOES HIS THING

The Albert Hall extravaganza would be discussed and dissected for decades. But in a more immediate sense, it shined a light on an emerging art form. Which would translate into poets being in demand at an ever-increasing pace. Clubs featuring poets and poetry/jazz combos were popping up like mushrooms. And along with those pluses was the fact that poets were, and musicians were now getting paid better and, yes, by degrees treated as professionals. "Touring became fairly constant," Brown reflected in *White Rooms & Imaginary Westerns*. "I didn't have to hitchhike all the time. Promoters would even pay for transport to get you to the gig on time."[42]

And Brown was getting his share of the gigs. A series of one-off gigs with singer/guitarist Davy Graham in and around Sheffield. That year's Edinburgh Festival, the Commonwealth Poetry Festival. Brown gladly plunged into the poetic/rockstar life, meeting and hanging out with fellow creatives, enjoying the attention of women and consuming much drink and drugs through the remainder of 1965 and into 1966. Brown's popularity and ego knew no bounds, the occasional gigs with Michael Horovitz, in hindsight, seemed almost quaint and from another time.

Into 1966, Brown came to the decision that it was time to part company with his long-time mentor. Brown put the breakup rather succinctly and in somewhat simplistic terms in conversation with the author when he said, "At one point Horovitz and I had a falling out."

But upon further examination, the 'falling out' was almost expected. Brown had long championed his natural anarchistic nature, his aversion to a long-term relationship of any kind and the manic drive to be in control. Given those qualities, the split between Brown and Horovitz had been inevitable.

And given those traits, it was not surprising that Brown almost immediately cast about for the musicians that would fill-out his very first band, Brown Poetry. Brown Poetry, fronted by Brown and a line-up that included Laurie Morgan (drums), Tony Roberts (saxophone) and Ron Rubin (bass) was, by all accounts, a short-lived and largely obscure first step for Brown who, in conversation with the author, was hard pressed to come up with particulars. "I had a group of very young musicians and we were trying to do some different things with saxophones. Nothing was actually recorded or released. We did end up doing an experimental television program for the BBC that was never shown."

Brown soon moved on to a more planned out notion with the formation of The First Real Poetry Band, the sole purpose of being able to read his work accompanied by free form electronic jazz. The band, which included future axe great John McLaughlin (guitar), Binky McKenzie, who replaced original bassist Danny Thompson who joined Pentangle, Laurie Morgan (drums) and Pete Bailey (Percussion).

But even as The First Real Poetry Band was rounding into shape, Brown recalled at various points in the websites *Please Kill Me.com* and *Music For The Head And Heart.com* and Cherry Red TV that he was a bit intimidated, "I had thought about properly singing about the time I formed The First Real Poetry Band. The initial concept was that I would do semi-improvised poetry over their jazz music. Because everybody in the band were such great musicians, I was terrified of actually singing with them."[43]

Brown's concerns aside, The First Real Poetry Band would prove quite the attraction, in places like The Middle Earth Club and The Marquee Club between 1966-67, with their musical approach fitting right in with the wave of psychedelia sweeping the UK. "We were less bebop and quite electric," explained Brown in a Cherry Red TV interview. "What we were doing was quite far out. When we played live, it sounded like we were from Mars."[44]

The First Real Poetry Band would have what Brown would consider a solid, polished ensemble," playing concerts, festivals and clubs. "We were doing some very interesting stuff. It was a professional thing."

When not performing live, The First Real Poetry Band, guided most likely by Brown's obsession with landing a record deal with every group he played with, were regularly in the studio, recording a series of demos that would dutifully be shopped around to labels who, while impressed with the band and their music, labels were unanimous in saying thanks but no thanks and would pass on signing them.

In a sense, Brown knew what the problem was and the problem was, indirectly him. "People were getting deals so I submitted some tapes with me reading my poetry while the band played," he said in a Cherry Red TV interview. "I tried that for a bit and gradually began to realise that the problem was that I was not a singer. So I said 'okay, I guess I'm going to have to start to sing'."[45]

Brown had long been keen on expanding his musical vocabulary as both a singer and an instrumentalist. He recalled attempting to learn the trumpet but it proved a struggle. As The Last Real Poetry Band chugged along through 1966-67, Brown began to entertain the idea of becoming a songwriter, buoyed by his recent success with Cream. He would begin playing around with some non-Cream like songs and would commit them to tape, complete with what Brown felt were only demo quality vocals. Which he proceeded to give to give to his good friend and mercurial blues/jazz musician Graham Bond.

"I sent Graham the demo recordings with me singing and, to my way of thinking I was not a great singer," he told this author. "After he listened, I told him that I was not a great singer. But Graham said but you just did sing. So I thought maybe I should start singing this stuff."

# BROWN GETS CREAMED

Upon its formation in 1966, Cream was immediately a band of legendary proportions. The musicians all had a legitimate pedigree in a number of notable bands. The concept of heavy blues and psychedelia was a potent musical weapon in conception. Cream had super group written all over it. There was just one fly in the ointment.

Cream was a rush job pure and simple.

Ginger Baker approached Eric Clapton early in 1966 with the idea of forming a classic power trio that would explore the world of blues/jazz. Clapton, who was then riding high as a reigning rock god on the strength of The Yardbirds and John Mayall's Blues Breakers, liked the concept and agreed to the concept in principle. But there was just one caveat.

Clapton strongly suggested that Jack Bruce be added on bass and vocals. Dealing with Bruce, with whom he had a long standing and often bitter feud dating back to Alexis Korner's Blues Incorporated and The Graham Bond Organisation days, was initially a hard pill to swallow, he would recall in his autobiography *Ginger Baker: Hellraiser*.

"I thought 'oh Jesus no.' But I said I'd think about it. I should have said no straight away but I didn't and so I agreed to give him another chance. We sat down and had a cup of tea and I said, 'I'm starting a band together with Eric, let's let bygones be bygones and try again.' Jack agreed to do it."[46]

Reluctantly, and at Baker's insistence, Robert Stigwood was brought aboard to manage Cream. Reluctant in the sense that Stigwood had a pop, commercial, money attitude about music that ran contrary to the attitudes of the band members who, initially, felt that the band would be truer to the art of it all if they managed themselves. Plus, truth be known, Stigwood did not have a clue as to what Cream was all about.

For that matter, neither did the band according to Clapton in his autobiography *Clapton*. "Musically, we didn't really have a plan. I never discussed a musical direction with the others because I didn't really know how to verbalise those concerns. We were struggling to find a direction."[47]

And what the band quickly discovered was that, in Robert Stigwood, Cream was being driven from the word go by the ultimate mercenary. Nobody was more aware of that then Bruce who laid out his feelings in no uncertain terms in conversation with *Guitarist Presents The Blues Magazine*. "From the beginning, Robert Stigwood was thinking 'Let's milk this for all its worth because it ain't going to last.' His attitude was 'Let's get them out there and make them play every toilet in the US for as long as they'll last before they go barmy or kill each other."[48]

Brown, who was not even in the Cream universe yet but he would prove a quick study when it came to Stigwood as he recalled in *The Guitarist Presents The Blues Magazine* interview. "The management never thought it (Cream) would spread. They never thought that we'd have hit songs. They had no bloody idea."[49]

Consequently, when Cream made their first official concert appearance on 29th July 1966 at The Twisted Wheel in Manchester, Cream had few if any songs to showcase as Clapton recalled in his memoir *Clapton*. "We only played three songs before we ran out and Ginger made the announcement that there were no more numbers. We played a couple of them over again but nobody seemed to care. Then we just jammed and the audience went crazy."[50]

The band seemed to care. With no identity to hang their hat on at that point and the prospect of a career playing amped up blues standards not too appealing. The members of Cream turned to an outside creative source, Pete Brown.

Bruce, as quoted in the Ray Coleman biography *Clapton*,

explained what he recalled as the particulars of the odyssey that led Cream and Pete Brown to cross paths. "When we (Cream) were jamming and working on riffs during those first rehearsals, I felt that we had to get someone in who could write song lyrics. Pete Brown immediately came to mind because, before forming Cream, I had some gigs at the St. Pancras Town Hall that were called Jazz And Poetry. The poets would come up and read their work in front of an audience. Pete Brown was one of the poets I really liked."[51]

Brown would only speculate as to why Cream suddenly had him on their radar when he told *Guitarist Presents The Blues Magazine* "I suppose they felt that I had a lot of chops as a writer. I was a well-known poet and I wrote and practiced a lot."[52]

This is where things get a bit dicey as to what happened next.

Who made that fateful call to Brown? Smart money and Brown himself say that it was Baker who made the initial offer to help Cream out lyrically. Some said that it was Bruce who made the first overture. The sure bet was that Clapton had nothing or very little to do with it. What finally emerged was two equally plausible versions of the night that Pete got Cream(ed).

First up the recollections of the late Cream bassist and songwriter Bruce who in the booklet accompanying the *Disraeli Gears* DVD recalled the night Pete and Ginger stopped by Bruce's flat for a bit of songwriting. "Pete and Ginger were at my flat trying to work on a song but it wasn't happening. My wife Janet then got with Ginger and they wrote a song called 'Sweet Wine' So I went off with Pete in another room and we started writing and it turned out that we had much better chemistry then Pete had with Ginger."[53]

Brown's version as told to this author is, by degrees, less dramatic but seems to jibe with the straightforward, no-

nonsense nature of the players. "Ginger had heard me doing stuff and I met Jack who was rooming with a musician friend of mine, John Mumford, So I went around, met Jack and everybody was quite sociable. After that, when Cream began to shape up and they knew I could write. So Ginger called me up and said the band was in a studio right around the corner from where I lived and said 'You want to come around and write some words for us?' And that was how it started."[54]

But Brown would recall in *All About Jazz.com* that, initially, he was cautious upon meeting them for the first time. "They were all very intelligent guys and I wondered why they would need anybody else."[55]

But Brown's seemingly non plussed reaction to Cream's offer was, he revealed to the author in understated tones, nothing less than life changing. "I think I was quite pleased. Part of me was wanting to get close to musicianship and musicians in general for quite a while. I felt I should give a real go at this."

The studio would be literally a quick walk around the corner that Brown made in a matter of minutes. After a quick 'how's it going mate', he quickly discovered that the members of Cream were all business. Bruce played back the music track a couple of times so Brown could capture the vibe of the song that would be 'Wrapping Paper'. It would be Cream's official first single, its first, albeit modest chart hit and would predate Cream's first album, *Fresh Cream*, but it would not be Brown's finest lyrical moment.

"In hindsight, what I contributed lyrically didn't work for me," said the ever-critical Brown to the author. "I was involved in my head with film music and poetry. I guess I overdid it. The band weren't quite sure what they were doing with it. If you listen to the song now, it has kind of like a Peter Green song for early Fleetwood Mac feel to it. But the thing that came out of 'Wrapping Paper was a very good chemistry between Jack and myself. Bottom line, I wrote the lyrics in less than a day and that's what got on the record."

With the marginal success of 'Wrapping Paper', Cream's management, The Robert Stigwood Organisation, seemed immediately intent on putting Cream on the rock and roll hamster wheel of record, tour and record again. And, by August with the band's debut album, *Fresh Cream*, already slotted for December, were looking for a second, quick strike single to prime the pump for the album. Cream once again turned to Brown for something quick and commercially dirty. Even at the early stages, Brown had a keen eye about what writing for Cream was going to be like.

"At the time, I didn't think of it being on call at a moment's notice," Brown told the author. "I was lucky that I could do things quickly. Not to say that I wouldn't have liked some more time on certain things because I would. It just so happens that I got lucky and that some things just fell into place. But I remember that the band's management was being very silly about the situation. It would have been more productive to put me on the road with the band so I could pick out ideas and present them to the band rather than waiting until they got off the road for a couple of days and ending up writing in a studio or a hotel room."

Brown had always had it in his creative DNA to write things fast so quick turnarounds was not necessarily a problem and, in the case of 'I Feel Free', which by degrees was superior to 'Wrapping Paper' and more in keeping with the vibe that Cream was trying to present, still had the hooks and musical bells and whistles of commercial radio pop of the day. The swift pace of writing the song was made all the easier by the fact that, by this time, Brown and Bruce were working like a well-oiled songwriting team. "'I Feel Free' was done quite fast," said Brown. "By that time, Jack and I had sat down a few times and worked things out. I believe I wrote the lyrics quite quickly. The music was already laid out. We didn't labour too much over it."

'I Feel Free', while a last-minute deletion from the *Fresh Cream* album, did have quite a bit of success as the band's second single, topping out at No. 11 on the UK singles charts and No. 116 in the US as a prelude to the American release of *Fresh Cream* (which did include the song as an album cut).

For Pete Brown completists, the song 'Wrapping Paper' would appear on the Scandinavian release of *Fresh Cream*. 'I Feel Free' and 'Wrapping Paper' would be Brown's only appearances on *Fresh Cream* which was largely composed of revamped traditional blues classics and a handful of collaborations between Bruce and his wife/writing partner Janet Godfrey.

Brown would celebrate the release of *Fresh Cream* and his ascendency to songwriter for one of the most hyped bands on the planet in Cream in a state of creative bliss. Word had gotten around both the rock music and the poetry community that Pete Brown was suddenly the flavour of the moment, despite Brown's self-effacing assessment that he was now merely a C+ celebrity.

While Cream would celebrate the New Year on what was quickly turning into the tour that never ends, Brown was a man of relative leisure, doing the occasional pick-up club gigs, hanging out, partying and getting his fair share of the girls. Brown would concede in the book *White Rooms & Imaginary Westerns* that "During this very unreal period, it was sex and dancing that kept me anchored to whatever reality I could muster."[55]

As it would turn out, Brown's 'reality' would be short lived, for both Cream and Brown. By March 1967, the Cream tour had reached the inevitable bump in the road. The individual members were beginning to get a bit frayed around the edges, album sales for *Fresh Cream* continued strong but had reached a point where the band was beginning to get not too veiled missives from management to let them know that it was about that time to get back into the studio and record some new songs. The call went out for Brown. It was time for Jack and him to get together and make some magic.

Bruce and Brown picked up pretty much where they left off with a demo containing 'Weird Of Hermiston', 'Clearout', 'Theme For An Imaginary Western', 'Look Now Princess' and 'SWLABR'.

Of that initial offering, management would reject all but 'SWLABR' on the grounds that they were too weird. Brown's anti-establishment leanings would rear its conspiracy head at the mention that the respective managements of Cream and Jack Bruce when it came to the decision to reject those early Cream demos (although they would all later appear in various compilations and collections).

"Cream's management (Robert Stigwood) claimed that the demos were either accidently or deliberately lost," an exasperated Brown told the author his theory. "Of course Jack's manager was a complete asshole who knew nothing about music and he hadn't liked what Jack and I had been writing."[55]

As for those songs that would make the cut, Brown would have fond memories. And one did not have to delve too deeply into that granddaddy of creative 800-pound gorillas to realise that 'Sunshine Of Your Love', is a song that continues to this day as the perfect combination of cinematic and earthy influences coupled with powerful tones and, dare we say it, commercial appeal. If there is such a thing as a classic 'Sunshine Of Your Love' is it.

Brown recalled in a *Songfacts.com* interview how Bruce and he captured lightning in a bottle with 'Sunshine Of Your Love' after a hard night at the office. "We had been working all night and had gotten some stuff done. We had very little time to write for Cream but we happened to have some spare time and Jack came up with a riff and said 'what about this then' and he played the famous riff. At that point, I looked out the window and wrote 'it's getting near dawn'. That's how it happened. It's actually all true."[56]

In a recent conversation with the author, Brown would delve deeper into the song and what it meant to him personally. "For me, 'Sunshine Of Your Love' was just a straight ahead song. I recall that it was the first song where I started singing myself. I was never quite sure what the song was really about until I started singing it. Then I realised that it was late and I was coming back from a gig and my girlfriend or wife was waiting up for me. It was the universal musicians storyline."

Brown has always found inspiration and influence in his everyday life. Good, bad or indifferent, he has seemingly always found that nugget, that scrap of something that has set his mind into overdrive. But nobody was more surprised than Brown when easily one of the most down periods in his life resulted in one of Cream's most memorable songs. 'White Room'. "It was a miracle that it all worked," he acknowledged in *Reason To Rock.com*. "It was me writing a monologue about being in a new flat and dealing with a depression and hopelessness."[57]

The fuel for what turned a less than idyllic lifestyle into 'White Room' was a watershed moment in 1967 in that Brown was, among other things, trying to come to terms with a relationship that appeared to be going off the rails while at the same time trying to give up both alcohol and drugs. While, almost after the fact, attempting to write lyrics for what had become one of the biggest bands in rock. And yes there was that little matter of a white room.

Brown was candid in conversation with the author about his emotional state of mind in conversation with Songfacts. com and with the author. "It was a transitional period for me.

I was in a meandering relationship. I was really broke and I was sleeping on people's floors and I was drinking and doing drugs. Then, in 1967 things began to turn around. Then I got a room in an apartment that belonged to a friend of a friend. It was a transitional period when I lived in an actual white room and where I tried to come to terms with various things and I stopped those things. I gave up all drugs and alcohol. It was a watershed moment."[58]

And it was a time when he continued to work at a prolific pace on new Cream music.

It was creative therapy of a kind and it was not an easy process. Bruce had some music and was looking for lyrics. In line with his current mental and emotional state, Brown responded with some lyrics about a doomed hippie girl, full of depression and dark thoughts called 'Cinderella's Last Goodnight'. Bruce, always a headstrong, opinionated type, rejected the lyrics out of hand. Undaunted, Brown, in a quite literal sense, returned to something revealing and emotionally taxing, an eight-page poem called *White Room* that encapsulated every element of a downward spiral wrapped around a description of the white room he was then living in, a dreary set piece of Brown literally baring his soul. Brown felt that he had something in *White Room* the poem but that it needed some work.

"It was a poem that needed something to make it into a song," reflected Brown in conversation with the author. "It was a very big poem and so there I was looking for a lyric hook for 'White Room' and I thought back to my days in journalism school where I had learned about phrasing and the idea of turning lines of poetry into verses. So I got that out in the poem and Jack loved it."

While 'Sunshine Of Your Love' and 'White Room' remain the longstanding hallmarks of Cream's legacy, there would be a lot of lesser but equally enticing kernels that rose out of the Jack Bruce/Pete Brown collaborations during the three years of Cream's existence. Easily one of the most playful and spirited entries into the often-serious nature of the Cream oeuvre was 'SWLABR'. The song is a straight-ahead romp with tough minded instrumental riffs mixed in with Brown's apparent fascination with psychedelic images.

Brown was feeling a bit sheepish when discussing the tale of a woman who has a lover by day and a lover by night. "The lyrics definitely have a psychedelic feel to them although, not having taken psychedelics I couldn't honestly tell you what psychedelic lyrics are. I do know that the lyrics are very misogynist. The song is about someone whose girlfriend has given him the elbow and he's going around town defacing pictures of her. 'SWLABR' is about the war between men and women. It's like drawing a moustache on the Mona Lisa. It's the blues and the blues has always been around the war between the sexes."

'Dance The Night Away' may well have been the most below the radar, subversive look at Brown's inner demons that, if one listens closely, form a very telling core of the album *Disreali Gears* which goes a long way toward establishing Brown as a viable fourth member of Cream and somebody who has not been afraid to look at himself in the mirror.

An alternately wrapped smartly around Bruce's very haunting vocals and Clapton's attention to more guitar emotion than histrionics, 'Dance The Night Away' is a powerful lyrical mixture of catharsis and angst, mixed smartly with subtle but necessary pop elements. And while Brown could make a case for the song being a lesser effort, he was quick to let this author know, it was, by degrees, emotionally important. "'Dance The Night Away' was one of those songs that helped me. I was not in great shape, what with the booze and drugs and one of the things that helped me get through all my stuff was dancing and having sex and, when I wrote these lyrics that was what the song was about to me."

When it came to the song 'Politician', Brown was thinking of addressing a far more real world issue, the political and sexual rise and fall of Secretary of State for War John Profumo. "I wrote the lyric first," he told *Please Kill Me.com*. "Originally it was a spoken word piece but I showed the lyric to Jack who had already written the music. It ended up all fitting quite well."[59]

Brown's fairly insulated songwriting duties with Bruce had largely kept him in the dark when it came to the ongoing tensions between Baker and Bruce who would often clash over musical as well as personal decisions. But by the time *Disreali Gears* was set to be released, Baker began to turn his anger to the fact that, because of their songwriting duties, Bruce and Brown were making more money in Cream than Clapton and Baker were. Brown would grow to sense that there was some tension afoot over the distribution of creative money. If there was any sort of tension between Brown and Clapton, Brown was not aware of any and insisted from the beginning that Clapton was fine with him writing the songs. But Baker was a whole other story as witness his rant in his autobiography *Hellraiser*.

"What I could see even at that time was that Jack Bruce and Pete Brown were earning more money out of Cream than Eric and I. I had formed the band and I had wanted Eric. I got Jack into the band by trying to be nice and all of a sudden, he and Pete Brown had taken over the writing. I thought this was incredibly unfair and still do."[60]

Brown has always been known as somebody with a thick skin when it came to personal and professional attacks. But when the attacks from Baker continued well into 1967, even the normally laidback Brown had finally had his fill. "I basically had it up to here and I told him as much not long before he died," reflected Brown. "I told him 'Look! When you first started Cream, if you had wanted to give me one quarter share of the bloody royalties, then you should have said so.' I was completely green about the business and wouldn't have known what I should have gotten."

But Brown would eventually wise up to the cutthroat nature of the music business and in particular, the wildly unethical antics of Robert Stigwood. Brown would get the hint when he visited Stigwood at his office to discuss his royalty issue as well as Stigwood's suggestion that Brown should sign with his publishing company. At one point in the conversation, Stigwood asked Brown how much of a royalty payment he should get for the song in question. Brown did not have a clue but pulled what would be a particularly low figure out of the air. Stigwood promptly ordered his secretary to issue a cheque in the amount Brown had requested. By the time Brown had stepped out of Stigwood's office he knew that he had made a mistake.

Brown, with more than a sense of irony in his voice, confessed to the author that "I had never been really great with the business side of music but I did quickly figure out that Stigwood was a crook and that I would not sign with him. I went out and got my own publishing deal and I've been getting fair royalties ever since. That's how I was able to finally buy a home. Getting my own publishing deal was probably one of the smartest things that I ever did. Up to that point I didn't realise that there was all kinds of money to be made from these things."

Cream would continue what had become a literal rock and roll grind midway through 1968. But the cracks in the less than three-year-old band were becoming evident. The tension between Bruce and Baker were the at large speculation for the demise of Cream. But the constant touring and recording, the inherent boredom of the road and, reportedly, more than a little substance activity, could also be chalked up as contributing factors.

But as the band, good soldiers to the end, finished off a final slate of tour dates and the appropriately titled final album, *Goodbye Cream*, Brown went about his business, landing a couple of final songwriting credits and bidding a fond farewell to the three-year stroke of luck that had catapulted him from little known, struggling poet to top of the mark rock and roll songwriter.

"I never saw much of Eric and Ginger in those later days," Brown recalled of those post Cream memories. "It wasn't the time to try and write with Eric because we had not really gotten to know each other that well. Ginger and I would go on and do a couple of things together that didn't go anywhere. Probably the best thing to come out of the Cream experience was that Jack and I had developed this tremendous chemistry that would continue on for quite some time.

It would be a period of treading water for Brown, trying at this and that and would include lyrical contributions to what many to this day consider Bruce's landmark album *Song For A Tailor*. But bottom-line Brown was looking for something going into the tail end of 1968 that would challenge him and that was, creatively, on point.

# BROWN ON ALCOHOL, DRUGS AND SEX... CLASS DISMISSED

To the casual observer, the songs 'White Room' and 'Dance The Night Away' were two Cream songs on divergent paths — one to legendary status and the other — to lesser known, but no less commendable, place in the Cream/Brown stable of songs. But to Brown, the two songs were much more important because, in 1967, they were two cornerstones of a long odyssey of vices that were coming to a close. "'White Room' and 'Dance The Night Away' were a couple of the very few songs about my life," he said to *Please Kill Me.com*. "During the time when I wrote those two songs, I was having a bad time."[61]

But before there were 'the hard times' Brown remembered being extremely cautious even as the sixties scene was evolving into a hallucinogenic free for all.

In an interview with the author as well as some insights supplied by *All About Jazz.com*, Brown was quick to reflect, given the tenor of the times, fanatic in wanting to become a part of the bohemian scene and all the cheap thrills that experience entailed. He was far from the stereotypical dope fiend. "I guess I had been drinking since about age fourteen and started getting into drugs in the early sixties. But I was more of a casual drug user than a hardcore addict. I had been drinking heavily, smoking dope and using speed for years. And I knew a lot of people at the time who were junkies (heroin) and a lot who were using LSD. Neither of those drugs had a place in my life. They looked much too frightening. I never knowingly took acid. I used to watch people doing it and I thought 'I don't want to be like that'."

Brown's casual but consistent alcohol and drug intake could not have come at a worst time in 1966-67. He was being pulled at a number of creative ends; working sporadically with The First Real Poetry Band (in the studios with demos and the occasional live gig), the constant and growing desire to become a full-time songwriter and the early success and challenges with Cream.

His desire to develop as a singer, the early stages of forming his own band, The Battered Ornaments and, at the never-ending desire to get his thoughts and words down for himself and, hopefully, for the masses. It was of that latter challenge in which his alcohol and chemical dependency were playing havoc. Brown would often hint at missed opportunities and chances because of his addictions and would go into some detail about his issues in a candid conversation with *Songfacts. com.*

"I did a lot of speed, alcohol during that period. But, in fact, when I was in that particular state my writing was not very good. I used to stay up for long periods of time when I was on speed and a lot of what I wrote when I was stoned, to be honest, was crap. I would not begin writing good stuff until I gave up doing all that stuff. I was discovering that to be a songwriter you're dealing with deadlines and all sorts of things so you have to be relatively efficient. It would take me a while to be able to do that."[62]

Brown's 'come to Jesus' moment would happen in 1967 when he was on the verge of writing what would become Cream's legendary songs. There was still enough time to hang out and get high and, as Brown would offer in conversation with this author when he chronicled the true horror of crashing.

"It was after a gig with Graham Bond. I ended up at a place where there were a lot of people I really didn't know. I ended up smoking something that apparently had a little extra ingredient in it. All of a sudden, I collapsed, became paralysed for about two hours. During this time I couldn't move and I was having these awful visions of my brains coming out of my nose, ears and mouth. I couldn't fucking move. Eventually I came back to more or less normal, thought that the whole experience was horrible but I thought 'okay' and tried to carry on. But every time I tried to have a smoke or drink, I started to get the shakes and the horrors. I thought maybe my body was trying to tell me something. I stopped pretty raw right then and there."

But 'raw' in Brown's memory did not necessarily equate with the notion of going cold turkey in the classic sense. For the first couple of weeks after deciding to give up alcohol and drugs, Brown would continue to experience reminders of his years of abuse. "I would have fits of panic attacks and claustrophobia," he told the author. "I couldn't go down in the underground for about four years. I couldn't go to the cinema for a whole year. But that was the period where I started the whole music thing and that helped an awful lot. I don't know what would have become of me if I didn't have the music. It was very healing, and it gave me something to concentrate on. It all helped a lot and eventually it came out on the other side of things."

Brown has always been fond of noting that one of his literary idols, Nathanael West, when famously asked what made him want to be a writer, West responded by saying in a *Music For The Head And Heart.com* interview "Well I was hoping that it would make me more attractive to women. There was that motivation of course."[63]

Although a bit behind the times with that axiom, Brown when it came to literary prowess and sexual ardour, was very much in lockstep with his much-adored mentor. "The poetry thing was very interesting at the time (the early sixties). Being a young man and very interested in the opposite sex was very good for that sort of thing."

Brown is very candid in admitting that he was a sexual babe in the woods in conversation with the author. He did not lose his virginity until he was twenty-one. "I was such a late starter sexually. Then I began to make up for lost time. I wanted to have as much sex as I could. I did like women very much. I didn't think much about contraception at the time. In those days, people started to find sexual freedom. It was a good time for a lot of people until bad things started to happen. People were having too much sex and were starting to get careless."

Brown sheepishly stated that he was among the "too much sex and getting careless faction" of the sexual revolution. "There were very wild times," Brown offered in an email exchange with the author. "I had no idea what I was doing and didn't always keep it covered."

The result being was that, by 1967, when Brown was flying high with Cream, he discovered, as chronicled in *White Rooms & Imaginary Westerns*, that he had taken missteps to huge heights. "I certainly needed to work. Two of my girlfriends were pregnant and both children, a boy and a girl, were born within a short time of each other. In my defence, I can only say that both children were wanted by their mothers, and I did my best trying to support them. I was not in love with either girl and their lapses in the relationships. Jessica, my daughter, is one of my best friends. For various reasons, I never became close with my son and I don't feel great about it."[64]

# BROWN GETS BATTERED

By the time the dust had officially settled on the short-lived history of Cream in July 1968, Brown was already full bore. He had, periodically, been in contact with the members of The First Real Poetry Band and would try on several occasions to get their demos into the right hands.

"We had done The First Real Poetry Band demos and nobody picked up on them," reflected Brown to the author. "It was frustrating because I always thought the boys in that band were such great musicians. So one day I thought why don't we put together a band?"

For Brown, the decision was not as cut and dried as all that. Brown, who at the time had begun spreading his wings beyond mere frontman/poet to attempts at percussion and trumpet, still harboured the notion that the only roadblock to the long-sought record deal was a capable singer. Which, in all candour, he continued to insist he was not, in an interview with this author. "I was a terrible singer, and I knew it."

But he liked the notion of putting together a band that he would create and would be creatively and professionally his, and would initially go under the moniker of Pete Brown & The Battered Ornaments. Putting a band together was not that difficult. Brown knew musicians who were either up to the challenge or knew people who were. Among them was sax player and long-time friend from the Alexis Korner/ Marquee Club days, Dick Heckstall-Smith. Brown's call sheet was also headed up by guitarist Chris Spedding who responded with his memories during a Q&A email interview.

"*The Battered Ornaments* were a bunch of jazzers, with the exception of drummer Rob Tait who was more of a rocker. My memory was that the band was being put together by Dick Heckstall-Smith for Pete. Pete lived close to me at the time and there were a bunch of us who hung out together including the two horn players Henry Lowther and Lynn Dobson."[65]

Pete Brown & The Battered Ornaments evolved in a timely manner; with another Brown fellow traveller George Kahn bringing along his reed instrument talents; initial percussionist Jamie Muir (who would be replaced early in the process by Pete Bailey and bassist Butch Potter. And after helping Brown recruit much of the band, Heckstall-Smith decided to join the party on sax. Charlie Hart on keyboards would round out what would be that promising line-up. Brown was thrilled with the musicians and the possibilities of the music.

But at the end of the day Battered Ornaments was, lyrically and musically, very much Brown's baby. The lazy man's critique would pass it off as a mixture of blues, soul mixed with folk, psychedelia and serious folk and avant-garde elements. Brown, in hindsight in *Strange Brew.com* and *Music Guy 247.com* was serious yet thoughtful about what came out of the Battered Ornaments library. "There were a number of different musical directions and influences. There was a lot of folk, blues quite a bit of jazz and some funky jazz. The songs I wrote for Battered Ornaments were very much of the time. Often I would write a song and decide 'okay, I like the sound of that but I don't always know what the song is about.' I've always been into good music so where ever it was I went. Consequently there's all sorts of influences in the Battered Ornaments music."[66]

Spedding's assessment was a lot more succinct. "We were trying to play rock but with a free jazz sound. We liked to think of ourselves as experimental and anarchistic."[67]

Whatever one's interpretation of the band's sound was, one thing was certain. Everybody loved it. Whatever 'it' meant. The word of mouth on Pete Brown & The Battered Ornaments was nothing less than staggering and in a positive way. Especially when the pedigree of the band resulted in, to Brown's way of thinking, unprecedented interest from the dollars and cents people. Brown, in *White Rooms & Imaginary Westerns*, described the windfall this way. "The Ornaments became relatively popular quite fast, either because of, or despite, there being nothing quite like us around."[68]

Whatever the reason, The Battered Ornaments quickly caught the attention of influential management firm Blackwell Enterprises whose muscle in the business almost immediately landed what, for Brown, was the holy grail, a record deal with Harvest Records, a well-respected haven for fringe and underground artists who would, shortly after *The* Ornaments signing, go uptown with the signing of Pink Floyd and Deep Purple.

It was all looking rosy for the band except for that one lingering doubt. Who was going to sing the songs? Brown had shown a reluctance to take over singing duties quite simply because he did not see his vocals up to the task. But, with the rare musical contribution of Spedding, he was the one writing the songs. But shortly before an ever expanding and potentially lucrative tour was shaping up, the band members had a sit down with Brown who recalled that moment in *All About Jazz.com*. "They said 'none of us can sing and you wrote the songs so you can fucking sing them. So I was stuck with it. Quite honestly, I was thrown in at the deep end."[69]

But once the band began touring, the downside of Brown's vocals was replaced by a sense of accomplishment and, yes, ego as he recalled in conversation with both the author and in *White Rooms & Imaginary Western*. "Before I knew it we were on the road. We did a lot of gigs and the tour proved to be quite successful. It was great being on the road and doing music, no matter how badly I sang. I was arrogant. I had a record deal and a band and I thought I could wing it."

It was sadly a constant sense of frustration that being on the road with Battered Ornaments was now putting a crimp in Brown's active love life. For the first time, Battered Ornaments was his band and he was suddenly responsible for a lot more of the economic side of the music business than simply showing up on time and performing. A lot was on his shoulders when the band was touring which left little time to chase women. Brown bemoaned as much in *White Rooms & Imaginary Westerns* when he complained "When we stayed overnight in any one place, the accommodations had to be communal to cut down on expenses and personally I preferred a private love life."[70]

The first official Battered Ornaments release was a single entitled 'The Week Looked Good On Paper'. A fairly recent introduction, the song having originally been written for Graham Bond, it did little in the way of chart notice but set the stage for the album to come. The first actual album, *A Meal You Can Shake Hands With* was released in early 1969 and hit all the high progressive notes. Brown was an expressive ideal frontman, and his questionable singing added a bit of charm to the group's more progressive leanings. His vocals, as well as his so-so trumpet and percussion play, was often the butt of a running joke within the band which Brown took well. After all, who could argue with the fact that *A Meal You Could Shake Hands With*, was a bit of a minor hit.

And as the leader of The Battered Ornaments, nobody had any complaints. Spedding, who had the reputation for blowing up in the face of those who could not meet his musical expectations, recalled nothing but superlatives when it came to Brown in an email conversation.

"Pete was very easy to work with," recalled Spedding. "He asked me to get him some tunes so that he could write some lyrics to them which encouraged me to get started as a songwriter which I'll always be grateful for. I'm also grateful to Pete for recommending me to Jack Bruce for his album *Songs For A Tailor* which kickstarted my session man career."[71]

The record label and management were thrilled with the relative success of *A Meal You Can Shake Hands With* and there was already whispers that the upcoming Hyde Park Festival headlined by The Rolling Stones was interested in the band filling a support slot. All of which translated into full speed ahead as they continued to tour while finding bits and pieces of recording time that would result in a follow up album entitled *Mantlepiece*.

All of a sudden The Battered Ornaments were serious contenders on the scene which brought long simmering issues to the surface during the recording of some backing tracks at the famed Abbey Road Studios. Where Spedding recalled how Brown was shown the door, literally a handful of days before The Battered Ornaments were set to open for The Rolling Stones.

"We recorded the backing tracks for *Mantlepiece* at Abbey Road and started to get a bit frustrated by Pete's musical contributions. We considered that his singing and trumpet playing just were not cutting it. So the rest of the band had a democratic vote about what to do about Pete. Pete Bailey and Charlie Hart had drifted off by this point. George Khan, Butch Potter and myself voted to ask Pete to leave. Rob Tait abstained."[72]

The moment that the band members broke the news to Brown had a potential to be an emotional blood bath. What could be said other than the obvious irony of it all. Brown had created the band and had brought the musicians together. There was no doubt that, on a purely ethical level, it was not right. But Brown did not seem to hold more than a mild grudge when approached on the admittedly touchy subject by *All About Jazz.com*. "That was a big mistake because I had a good act. I was good on stage. But the rest of the band thought I was crap. Spedding had this thing that he eventually got rid of people. He did it with a lot of bands he had been in."[73]

As it turned out, the rock gods were definitely on Brown's side when it came to payback on the band mates who had unceremoniously dumped him and Spedding was upfront in conversation with the author about what happened after they dismissed him.

"We wanted to finish the album *Mantlepiece*. Butch grabbed a couple of the songs to put his vocals on and I was left with putting the vocals on the rest. We soon realised that not one of the remaining members of the band was any better at singing than Pete We hadn't thought that one through. Much of what I had to sing on that album wasn't even in my key. It was all very chaotic and the band started to fall apart Although I have to admit that *Mantlepiece* was fairly well received and actually quite good."[74]

And finally there would be one final bit of karma irony, the much talked about Hyde Park Rolling Stones appearance. "Pete had left the band some days or weeks before The Rolling Stones concert," said Spedding. "It was the band's first gig without him and I had broken my wrist by falling off a horse and so I ended up playing the show with my left arm in a cast. As I remember, it was quite good optics for a band called The Battered Ornaments."[75]

Spedding's career would be, indirectly, jump started when he reconfigured the balance of The Battered Ornaments contract, minus the remaining band members, into a two record solo deal with Harvest. The fallout from The Battered Ornaments debacle would not be so good for Brown. The Battered Ornaments, minus Brown, would remain for a time with Blackhill Management. As a bone, Blackhill would offer Brown a separate contract that would return him to 'just poet' status. Brown's response?

"I told them to get lost," Brown in no uncertain terms recalled in *White Rooms & Imaginary Westerns*. "They demanded money to release me from the contract. Naively, I gave them some money but not all they asked for. They were waving lawyers at me. Then they printed a picture of me in the company's in house magazine on a woman's body. I showed the magazine to my lawyer and he told me that there were grounds for defamation against Blackhill. That threat got me out of the contract and they never got the rest of the money."[76]

Brown was now officially on his own, admittedly a bit shellshocked by the betrayal but looking to upcoming projects as his way of getting even.

# THAT'S THE FACTS JACK

Jack Bruce had hit more highlights in his decades long career than one could shake the proverbial stick at. But journalistically tough and go face to face with the legendary singer/bassist/songwriter produces an obvious no brainer in response to his highest of career highs.

"When the songs that I wrote with Pete Brown were suddenly big hits, that for me was the highest of high points," Bruce reflected in conversation with *Brave Words.com*. "One day I was driving in a taxi in New York and one of our songs came on the radio, well it doesn't get any better than that."[77]

When one thinks of classic rock songwriting duos, the list is often fairly short. How can one top Lennon and McCartney and, running a very close second, Jagger and Richards. But for our purposes, it would be a crime against creativity to overlook the dynamic duo of Bruce and Brown, who, over the course of thirty plus years have been fairly low key in the trenches, with the possible exception of Cream duty, as Bruce and Brown: Songwriters at large. And as history points out, nobody has been quite certain who came first in the creative process.

As witness UK author Stephen Leigh's take on the matter in *Stephen Leigh.com uk* who saw things this way, way back in the day. "I remember going to a poetry reading in Liverpool in 1966 and Pete Brown was on the bill. Pete got up to read and said, 'I am going to read some poems but they are really lyrics for songs by a rock group called Cream'."[78]

Sometime in this search for absolute truth, Leigh asked Bruce about what Brown had said. The bassist was quick to set the record straight in the same Stephen Leigh report. "The music came first in almost all of the songs we did together. I would do the music and then Pete and I would sit down and hammer out the lyrics."[79]

As one can surmise, the creative love match between Brown and Bruce wasn't always sublime. Bruce had already developed a bit of a dictatorial/authoritarian reputation among musicians. His dust ups with the equally combustible Ginger Baker, who once pulled a knife on Bruce during a heated creative argument are legendary. And Brown, as he indicated in *White Rooms & Imaginary Westerns*, would acknowledge that Bruce could be hard to get along with both personally and professionally, when it came to their working relationship, Brown was in for the long haul.

In a conversation with Stephen Leigh, the late bassist made no bones about the fact that it was his way or the highway while casting a bit of shade on Brown and the Cream classic 'White Room'.

"I am very particular about what I sing, not just the meaning of the words but the actual sound of the words. I regard the actual sound of the words as an instrument and, to my way of thinking, certain words don't sing very well. For instance, the song 'White Room' started off as something about selling fridges to Eskimos, something very bizarre. Then Pete and I worked on it until we got what I wanted. Pete would write the words but I would throw in lines and words. That's the way we worked."[80]

To be certain, there would be tension in the air when Bruce called Brown up for a writing session and it was with a mixture of humour and practicality that they managed to keep the process going. Brown recalled as much in conversation with *Strange Brew.com*. "There was this chemistry and that's what sustained us. That was what was really happening. Jack could work very fast because he was so versatile. I could work very fast because we had to."[81]

Bruce, in *Ultimate Classsic Rock.com*, couched his reasons he liked Brown with more than a bit of tongue in cheek. "Yeah,

Pete and I were always a fixture. Pete always understood my Scottish suicidal music and he was always able to come up with some great lyrics. Pete was always very versatile when it came to getting words down."[82] He further explored the joined at the hip nature of his relationship with Brown in *Goldmine* when he offered "Pete seems to know me better than I know myself and sometimes that's pretty scary."[83]

When talking about Bruce, Brown would easily come down on both sides of Bruce's nature as he acknowledged. "I got on extremely well with Jack most of the time. We liked much of the same music and humour and our politics were similarly left wing. But Jack could be a bit spoiled sometime. Because of his immense talent, he never had to work a miserable day job."[84]

And of course, Brown was quick to point out in *All About Jazz.com*, that when Bruce and he were having one of those days, they were still able to function as a creative team. "I'm mostly pretty easy to get on with," said Brown. "Jack was always half and half so we had times when we didn't get on. But we always had that incredible creative chemistry to fall back on."[85]

Consequently, the chemistry between the two was strong as Cream played out its run. Brown's nature had always been to be up for anything and he was thrilled when Bruce rang him up early in 1969 with an offer he could not say yes to fast enough. Because Bruce could not run away from Cream fast enough.

He was looking to make a very song-oriented record, a more self-contained less jam-oriented album that would incorporate a wide variety of jazz and blues musicians and exotic instrumentation seemingly at odds with accepted musical forms. He was looking for more literary and esoteric lyrics, a more divisive tone that would defy simple categorisation. And, perhaps most importantly to the process of making *Songs For*

*A Tailor*, Bruce was, quite simply, looking for somebody who knew how he worked and was more than willing to go along for the ride.

"It was a natural process for us to continue to work together," Brown told *Strange Brew.com*. "There was that chemistry, and we already had a bit of success with Cream. We were already kind of known as a songwriting duo and so I guess the obvious thing to do was to carry on."[86]

*Songs For A Tailor*, recorded in April-May 1969, was immediately seen as a bit of a left turn for Bruce and Brown. A total of ten songs, with only one over five minutes in length with a couple of Cream rejects thrown in for good measure ('Weird Of Hermiston' and 'The Cleanout'), played very much to Brown's literary and sixties place in real time. But Brown insists that his lyrical contribution to the album was very much in keeping with the pair's creative sensibilities. "Jack's music was very compelling," he told *All About Jazz. com* "It was not abstract. I could see it as being full of images. It was almost like I was translating something."[87]

Observers looking for even a hint of creative issues between Brown and Bruce were disappointed. Brown wrote the lyrics to all of the songs, a well-known fact in most circles and Bruce took the sole composer's credit. To call it fair would be stretching it a bit. Brown would acknowledge in *White Rooms & Imaginary Westerns* that he did feel chaffed at the fairly unspoken pecking order that had quickly developed between the two musicians. "I was never quite sure where I stood with Jack. Deep down I realised I was working for him rather than being in a partnership. This was to surface frequently in our relationship, often souring it."[88]

But in *Songs For A Tailor*, as would be his contributions to future Jack Bruce albums, Brown would have his moments in the sun. A prime example on *Songs For A Tailor* would be what many critics would consider one of the greatest singles to never have charted and often recorded by the likes of Mountain and countless others, 'Tales Of An Imaginary Western', a powerful cinematic exercise that was the perfect melding of interests and influences.

And as Brown would explain in a *Songfacts.com* conversation, it was a textbook example of the give and take that drove Bruce and himself to a formula that worked. "'Theme For An Imaginary Western' was originally about Graham Bond. For me, The Graham Bond Organisation were like a mixture between pioneers and outlaws. When Jack played me the music, it reminded me of western film music which I have always been quite fond of and love. So I got a lot of the western film thing going in the lyrics. But then I thought no it was not about cowboys, it's simply about Graham Bond."[89]

The inclusion of the songs 'Weird Of The Hermiston' and 'The Cleanout', which had been summarily rejected by Cream's record label for not being commercial enough, were a welcome addition to *Songs For A Tailor*, both chugga-chugga style blues rockers replete with fairly blatant psychedelia courtesy of Brown. And truth be known, there was probably a bit of backatcha nose thumbing at both songs, in Bruce's presentation they were quite masterful album cuts.

*Songs For A Tailor* was released on 29th August 1969. Whether Bruce and Brown liked it or not, they both sensed what the reception would be. The comparisons and allusions to what Bruce did with *Cream* were inevitable, albeit unfair, with descriptions such as 'seminal' dotting the critical landscape that was generously considered 'mixed'. And Brown, by association, was not immune from unfriendly fire, with *Rolling Stone* weighing in with the opinion that the lyrics were unsuccessful, silly and overburdened by an overabundance of literary references.

Still, *Songs For A Tailor* would do respectable chart

business, reaching number 6 on the UK album charts and number 55 on the Billboard album charts. For his part, Brown was none the worse for wear for his second creative dance with Bruce.

Now he was on to the next.

## PIBLOKTO ANYONE

Piblokto. More anecdotal attachments then you can shake a stick at. But *White Rooms & Imaginary Westerns*, proved to be a fairly quick and succinct, drawing of Piblokto

Check out the Lawrence Ferlinghetti beat period novel *Her* and there is Piblokto, front and centre in all its glory. Speculation had it that Piblokto was in fact a period of sexual orgy during periods of solar eclipses in the Artic — a little translation of the Inuit language meaning Arctic Hysteria — which often resulted in bouts of hysteria and depression. In line with this, leave it to *Rolling Stone* to put the definitive take on Piblokto, tracking down a professor who, perhaps wisely, preferred to remain nameless in all this when he acknowledged that Piblokto was an itching disease common in Artic regions that could only be cured by exposure to the cold.[90]

It's most likely that Brown's state of mind after he was summarily dismissed from The Battered Ornaments and cast adrift was at ease. Thanks to the Cream money which was now coming in at a regular clip, Brown was, by his own estimation," reasonably wealthy at the time", and so was a creative man of leisure, reconnecting with a by now eclectic group of musicians that included Jim Mullen, Roger Bunn, Laurie Allen and Dave Thompson. Informal jamming quickly evolved into informal songwriting and, finally, the very formal announcement that Brown's Piblokto was officially a unit and in active rehearsals.

But Brown still harboured some psychological bruises from his dealings with management during the rise and fallout with Blackhill and was cautious about just handing over management and publishing to just anybody. Enter Gerry Bron, a producer as well as somebody hip to management and agency matters, who was persuaded to come and check out the band in rehearsal.

Bron was suitably bowled over, and a deal was struck that would put Bron in charge of Piblokto's agency and publishing fortunes. But Brown was no longer a babe in the woods when it came to the business and, as he recalled in *White Rooms & Imaginary Westerns* that he proceeded with caution. "I should have handed him the management as well, but I was too bruised by the Blackhill experience and kept it for myself."[91]

Brown also proved he was street wise when he continued to hold onto his contract, which made Harvest, who were still inclined to play the progressive card, the option to sign Piblokto to their label after listening to a band demo.

To the trained critical eye this seemed a generous step up from his The Battered Ornaments stint. Piblokto was much in the spirit of Ornaments but with a seemingly crunchier rock sound to go hand in hand with Brown's lyrics, which remained very much in the realm of poetic psychedelia. The songs, made up of an enticing mixture of prog rock, blues rock, jazz rock and a dash of folk, was solid commercially and creatively.

And the most amazing element of this new group was that Brown's vocals, very much in the vein of Jethro Tull's Ian Anderson on many cuts, but totally serviceable in tandem with the band, had suddenly emerged as fairly decent which, to Brown's way of thinking in *Strange Brew.com*, was still light years away from where he wanted it to be. "For a long time, I was still not a good singer. But I kept at it and, for the most part, it fit the type of music we were playing."[92]

And it was the type of music Piblokto was playing, more straight ahead prog rock with a heavy emphasis on soaring keyboard runs thar helped Brown manoeuvre his limited vocal skills. "I coped reasonably well the varied time signatures, although the more sophisticated harmonic approach caused some anxiety within the band some nights. In all honesty my pitch was kind of dodgy at that point."[93]

The quality of Brown's vocals would take a backseat with Piblokto as Bron would prove anxious and aggressive to make Brown's latest venture a success. Bron was working his ass off in getting Piblokto out on the road. By summer of 1969, Brown's second attempt at running his own band was on tour pretty much full time. It did not take long for Brown to assume the role of big boss man.

By Piblokto's very second gig, at the Lyceum, Brown was already dealing with a tough business decision. Drummer Laurie Allen showed up at the gig, fresh from a friend's wedding and very much out of it. The result was a terrible set that played havoc with the hard rocking set the band had laid, out as well rehearsed. There was a lot of anger in the air, made even more tense because of Allen's long-standing relationship with Brown.

But Brown recalled he did what had to be done. "I fired Laurie on the spot and got Rob Tait back from The Battered Ornaments who (as luck would have it) were dissolving. In the end, musically it made more sense — having Tait in the band gave more of a rock/rhythm and blues feel to the rhythm section."[94]

It soon became evident that Brown was fully capable of running a taut ship while allowing a fair degree of free spiritedness and chemical and alcohol fuelled high jinks. But at the end of the day Piblokto, going into the end of the decade, was a fairly hot commodity on the hip college circuit, averaging four to five well-paying gigs per week, by mid-level progressive rock standards and turning Brown's second attempt at fronting a band of his own designs into a band, fully capable of supporting itself. In short order, the band broke out of the UK and into the European market where the money vastly improved.

Piblokto was running hot, built for speed as a band,

management and the record label Harvest which truth be known, may have been trying extra hard on Brown's behalf to make up for The Battered Ornaments fiasco.

That Harvest wanted product out and fast was evident in October 1969 when, shortly after signing on the dotted line, Piblokto released its first single, 'Living Life Backwards', a tough-minded rocker b/w 'High Flying Electric Bird', a ballad laced with prog melodies. The single showcased several aspects of what the band, creatively, was up to and would pave the way for their first full length album *Things May Come And Things May Go But The Art School Dance Goes On Forever*.

The album, produced by Brown and whose title comes from Brown's long held enthusiasm for the post-war art schools who fuelled the creative advances well into the sixties, saw changes in the way Brown went about his business, perhaps still smarting from his Battered Ornaments days. *Things May Come And Things May Go But The Art School Goes On Forever*, is far more commercial sounding and mainstream, musically, than anything Brown had done to date. And the process allowed a certain amount of creative give and take with his fellow band members.

Brown's solo contributions ('Someone Like You', 'Firesong', and the title track '*Things* May Come And Things May Go But The Art School Dance Goes On Forever'), two songs with Mullen ('High Flying Electric Bird', 'Golden Country Kingdom') one with Bunn ('Country Morning') one by Brown, Mullen and Bunn ('Walk For Charity Run For Money') and one Battered Ornaments leftover co-authored with Chris Spedding ('Then I Can Go But Can I Keep').

The critical success of *Things May Come And Things May Go But The Art School Dance Goes On Forever*, drawing rave reviews and showing up on several best of the year rock lists, only served to push *Piblokto* to strike while the iron is hot. The departure of Bunn (replaced by Steve Glover) and the never-ending sense of restlessness within the band seemed to portend a band that might be rushing toward the precipice. Consequently, the first album had barely hit the streets when Brown and company were back in the studio, working helter skelter on the album *Thousands On A Raft*.

*Thousands On A Raft*, once again produced by Brown with a heaping helping of Mullen in the songwriting and instrumental side, was a different, albeit just as rocky, six song collection that included 'Aeroplane Head Woman', 'Station Song Platform 2', 'Highland Song', 'If They Could Only See Me Now Parts 1 and 2', 'Got A Letter From A Computer', and 'Thousands On A Raft', was a solid slice of jazz oriented rock with Brown's seemingly ever improving vocals and often a head of their time lyrics, striking a perfect balance with progressive instrumental edges.

While often considered the lesser of Piblokto's output, there was an inescapable sense and tension pulsing through the grooves, much of which most likely was caused by the fact the band was literally falling apart as the album was being made.

Tait had already given notice that he would be gone after the completion of *Thousands On A Raft*, Mullen had been made an offer from Brian Auger's jazz funk band *Oblivion Express* that was too good to pass up and, and, as for Thompson, he had quite simply decided that it was time to go. Logic dictated that with a new album out, it was time to get out on the road to promote it. But as *Thousands On A Raft* was already racking up good notices, Brown had one problem. With the mid 1970 addition of bassist Steve Glover and the subsequent non album single 'Can't Get Off The Planet' b/w 'Broken Magic' which essentially went down without a whimper…

Piblokto was suddenly a band in name only.

# PIBLOKTO IN DECLINE

Fortunately, Brown had a reputation and knew just about every musician in the business. And having two critically acclaimed albums and a solid history of non-stop touring did not hurt his recruiting efforts.

In short order, Mark II of the Piblokto line-up was filled out with the addition of keyboardist Phil Ryan, Brian Breeze on guitar and John 'Pugwash' Weathers on drums. Along with the new line-up, Brown took it upon himself to form a co-op arrangement with the band that would allow no upfront wages but would eliminate the need for a second travelling vehicle. This was very corporate on Brown's part and a move that would result in claustrophobia on occasion. Reading between the pronouncements, the decision also pointed to Brown as somebody who, after years of living hand to mouth for his art, had become a dollars and cents advocate and a bottom line guy.

Short term, the idea seemed to work as Piblokto's new line-up immediately embarked on a mammoth tour of Great Britain and France. The band also used this time to road test the new line-up in the studio when they recorded a single, 'Flying Hero Sandwich' b/w 'My Last Band'. Brown was thrilled when 'Flying Hero Sandwich' began getting great reviews, a considerable amount of radio play and was selling quite well. Thrilled with the prospect of a successful return for the band, Brown approached Harvest with the request for some promotional help.

The record company turned Brown down flat. For Brown, this slight was the proverbial last straw of his relationship with *Harvest*. But in the meantime, there was still more *Piblokto* to come. The band continued in a barnstorming tour of France, Germany, Scotland and Wales, piling up the fans as well as the inevitable rock and roll high jinks and mishaps. Things on the business front were up and down. Harvest had for all intents and purposes stopped putting any effort into marketing Piblokto and The Battered Ornaments material when they refused to submit both group's material for US distribution.

Brown had always been a realist. He could sense that, for all the talent and skills in the band, it could not prevent the group from what had turned into an inevitable slide to done and out. But even his dogged determination could not hold the second Piblokto line-up together.

The chemistry musically had been good. Put Breeze and Weathers on stage and they were like a well-oiled machine. Between Paris and the UK, the pair were a constant powder keg that was, more and more, going off. Finally the band combusted, with Breeze and Weathers up and leaving Piblokto and going their separate ways. Brown tried a few gigs with fill in musicians before throwing in the towel and looking for long term replacements. Drummer Ed Spevock and guitarist Taff Williams joined up and Piblokto III was once again up and running, concentrating on their strongholds of France and Germany.

Brown had long been a champion of anti-corporate attitudes but, as Piblokto essentially filled out its last round of performances, while awaiting what would be a failed attempt to get US distribution for Piblokto's music, Brown, at least to the band's current line-up, was now the enemy as he recalled in *White Rooms & Imaginary Westerns*. "Although the band was now co-operative, there was always a bit of a distance between us because of my relative wealth, even though it helped them. Phil and I had a number of confrontations on those last tours because he had spent his money on booze and dope."[95]

Stories began to surface in Piblokto's final days that a final, ultimately unrecorded album of new Piblokto music was in the works that would feature Brown, Williams and Spevock. If it was fact, nothing came of it. If it was fiction, it all came across as a last-ditch attempt at what was perceived by those in the know as a dying creative enterprise. Brown would put an official end to Piblokto in late 1971 when he retired the name.

Despite the potential of Piblokto Brown was disappointed with both the lack of creative success and, finally its demise. But he would not be choked up for too long as he had other issues to deal with. Most notably, the money he had made was beginning to trickle in at a regular pace which was exciting but also confounding as he would admit in a *Music For The Head And Heart* conversation.

"I've never been great with money and I made a lot of mistakes. When I first had money, I went crazy at one point. I didn't know what the fuck to do with it. I would drive around in mini cabs with my girlfriend and just spend money and buy anything. But that didn't last very long because I realised that wasn't the way to do it."[96]

# PETE THE POET

Pete Brown was always a poet, even before he knew he was a poet. That fact was very obvious to reviewer Kris Needs in *Record Collector* who, in 2016 would offer up a succinct appreciation of just what made Brown the poet tick. "Pete inhabits a world of his own making."[97]

In the best possible way, Brown has reflected his times, his past, his present, the now and into the future. His literary ammo belt full of satire, a wide-ranging sense of lyrical genius and always quick with the humour, the irony and variations on both. Brown addressed the dichotomy of his earliest poetry and the lyrics that were to come in *The Generalist.com* and *All About Jazz.com*. "The poetry I was writing early on can best be described in loosely musical forms like chase choruses. Theoretically, it was pretentious but what saved it was the humour and the Britishness."[98]

Brown's blueprint for his earliest poetry, starting in the mid-fifties up to the mid-sixties found an early home in *Evergreen Review*, *New Departures* and a signature anthology called *Children Of Albion: Poetry Of The Underground* which contained a total of fifteen of Brown's poems. All, as Brown offered in *Music Guy 247.com*, were quick and to the point. "I started out writing short kinds of things and then kind of progressed to other stuff."

His earliest works were very much of the time, a revolt if you will against tradition and mores in poetry and literature. "The poetry was all about the voice," Brown recalled of those early Bohemian days in *All About Jazz.com*. "It was a time of breaking down the walls with real voices."[99]

All of Brown's slim bibliography of poetry collections are tied to various moments when the poet with an already veteran status as a working poet and with decidedly jazz leanings was inching his way into the jazz scene and that fateful day when *Cream* came a calling. *Few Poems* includes short, sharp poetic jabs and feints at the establishment. Creative, social and political. It is rough, raw and hints at a sense of time and place that would become Brown's songwriting hallmark.

*Let 'Em Roll Down Kafka!* was released in 1969. By this time, Brown had arrived on the scene in a very big way and was paying some world-weary dues. The out of nowhere success with *Cream*, the on the job learning experience and ultimate indignities of The Battered Ornaments and the old college try with Piblokto had given Brown a moment to reflect poetically speaking with the realities and the struggles. But rather than a deluge of reality based biographical lines, Brown offers up a slim volume of powerful, often mystical asides to what he had written and, by association, read while coming of age in the sixties. There was an homage to the short, punchy elements of Kerouac which, by turns, are whimsical and pungent and never less than telling. Such as this slight bit.

**Reckless**
Last night I was reckless
Didn't brush my teeth
And went to bed tasting my dinner all night
And it tasted good

Later in the collection we dally with Brown the mystic and haunted poetry, reflective of time and place.

**The Old Cloth Cannot Dream Silk**
Here there is no slight sound
Of the clothes falling
To reveal the white body
The walls are slowly laughing themselves to dust
Sitting at attention
By the typewriter
The stone figure
Is beginning to sag

> The banknotes scamper
> Gay in the gutter
> And along the streets
> Until the rain
> And the wind wings cracked bells
> Far away

By the time *Let 'Em Roll Kafka!* was published, Brown was fully in command of the poetic form and would continue to effectively transition him from page poet to rock and roll lyricist.

# BRUCE AND BROWN BACK TO WORK

That Jack Bruce would ring up Brown when he was inspired to follow up *Songs For A Tailor* with another solo album, *Harmony Row*, dialling up Brown was barely an afterthought. Because whether they liked it or not, they were each half of a quite natural and rewarding whole.

Journalist Duncan Heining drew an effective blueprint of their relationship in *All About Jazz.com*. Brown's creative approach was marked by a distinctive style and imagery. He was fond of cowboys, science fiction, politics, love, loss and betrayal. All of which seemed to quite naturally mesh with Bruce's highly personal compositional style. And for Brown, the call could not have come at a better psychological moment.

The stresses and strains of piloting the last stages of Piblokto's up and down run, especially when it pertained with dealing with corporate and band management issues, was putting Brown in dire need of a less hectic bit of business. Bruce's offer seemed just what the doctor ordered. And what would be the challenge for Brown, as always, to get inside Bruce's head.

*Harmony Row* was based upon the basic power trio (bass, guitar, drums) but would be a jumping off point for more intellectual and literary forays on the songs 'Can You Follow', 'Escape To The Royal Wood (On Ice)', 'You Turned The Tables On Me', 'Mourning Story', 'Folk Song', 'Smiles & Grins', 'Post War', 'A Letter Of Thanks', 'Victoria Sage' and what many critics think was the album's standout track, 'The Consul At Sunset'.

That Bruce would resort to twists and turns was not a surprise to Brown. His work with *Cream* and *Songs For A Tailor* made him fully aware of how *Harmony Row* would roll. He knew how it would all work out in Bruce's world. Creatively Bruce would have the final say so and would, as before, take sole songwriting credits. But within that framework, Brown would also be allowed relatively free creative reign. All of which made *Harmony Row* a good trade off. And one that, given the parameters that Bruce had set up for *Harmony Row*, a perceived meandering collection of songs that ran the gamut from hard rock elements to a hybrid mixture of progressive rock and folk

Brown was given room to move in any number of directions and, according to Bruce in a *Classic Rock Review.com* interview it was a bemused Bruce who hinted what Brown had in mind. "Pete had this mad idea that the songs were like a big show on ice. He saw it as a kind of concept album in a way."[100]

Other observers saw a much deeper exploration of the album by Brown. *His Voice.com* speculated that Brown was using the occasion of *Harmony Row* to revisit the very elements of his past that had gotten him to that point, "What Brown was doing was taking Bruce's original compositions and incorporating impulses gained from British post war Beat poetry and surrealism."[101]

There would be a lot of speculation centred around the album as it neared its July 1971 release date. The kind of 'what is this about' and 'what are they up to' that would almost guarantee a degree of acceptance right out of the box.

But upon release, *Harmony Row*, good advance notice in many quarters aside, failed to chart. The answer may well lay in a review by Tony Palmer in the *London Observer* that damned the record amidst faint praise and a critical shout out to Brown. "The musicality is polished and exact. The spontaneity of the performance suffers a little. But that is a small price to pay for the skill of the recording. The music flows precisely out of the nuance of the words, their meaning inexplicably linked with the kinds of sounds produced. It's almost impossible to imagine the songs performed in any other way."[102]

For the working man ethic in Brown, *Harmony Row* was a job well done.

# GRAHAM BOND... DEAL WITH IT

Pete Brown had known Graham Bond long enough to know the legendary and, yes, notorious musician at his best and his worst.

First the best, a pioneering musician in the British blues and jazz rock scene who Brown would, at the drop of a hat, go to bat for as one of the most talented musicians on the planet. On a personal level, Bond could be encouraging, letting Brown know that he should try singing when nobody including Brown himself, gave Brown's vocal skills a fighting chance. If Brown never wrote another song, he would be forever enshrined for *Theme From An Imaginary Western* which he has sworn to this day was a paeon to Bond and the musicians who made up The Graham Bond Organisation.

To say that Brown was a dyed in the wool fan would be an understatement as witness his rose-coloured appreciation in *Classic Rock Magazine*. "I got the opportunity to see The Graham Bond Organisation play live a lot and absolutely adored them. There was nothing like them. They had a lot of spirit of jazz but with ferocious energy of blues and rock. Graham encouraged people. He'd always make you deliver something beyond what you thought you were capable of,"[103]

Now comes the tough part.

Bond seemed forever on a downward spiral, bedevilled by a seemingly self-destructive cycle of drugs, dark mysticism and a propensity for taking any moment of good professional venture and turning it into misadventure and disaster. Throw in various bouts of psychological, often violent behaviour that compared favourably with the worst episodes of Ginger Baker and it was no surprise that going into the end of 1971, Bond was in the latest bad patch and sinking fast.

Of this, Brown was equally candid in *Classic Rock*. "In the early days, Graham did seem relatively well adjusted but, when the heroin took hold, he got rather devious and difficult."[104]

Brown knew better but that didn't stop him from stepping in to salvage a friend and fellow musician. A couple of shakedown gigs around Christmas 1971. Bond had recently been sacked by Bruce for, among other things, being too drunk to hit the appropriate chords. But Brown, on the strength of those two gigs was encouraged. "There was good chemistry between us," reflected Brown. "It seemed to bode well. We would go forward together."[105]

Bond And Brown was born, the band ultimately filled out by Ed Spevock on drums and DeLisle Harper on bass. Brown knew what came next, put a band together, get a label deal, hit the road and record an album. The only difference being that, in the case of Graham, every waking moment had to revolve around the manic state of the singer, be it substance abuse, drug, alcohol and girlfriend issues and just plain unreliability from gig to gig. In the case of Graham, the ever patient and supportive Brown would find a personality who, quite simply, had no clue when it came to money and the handling of same.

When Bond & Brown formed, Graham was almost completely out of money and in danger of his wife and himself being evicted. In short order, and due largely to the efforts of Brown, he and Graham knocked out a respectable set of new material, landed a record deal, recorded literally two albums back to back, *The Lost Tribes* EP and the full length album *Two Heads Are Better Than One*, and then spent nearly all of 1972, touring big and small venues.

The album *Two Heads Are Better Than One* would definitely prove a potent calling card highlighting Bond's power when it came to traditional soul/blues/ funk and jazz while melding Brown's sixties penchant for psychedelia and pure poetic influences into a sturdy, enticing and, in the best possible way, a creative snapshot captured in time and relevance. *Two Heads Are Better Than One*, was light years better than Bond's dodgy history and showed that Brown could manoeuvre around any genre and come up smelling like a rose. At eight songs, 'Lost Tribe', 'Ig The Pig', 'Oobati', 'Amazing Grass', 'Mass Debate',' Looking For Time,' 'C.F.D.T. (Colonel Fright's Dancing Terrapins)' and 'Scunthorpe Crabmeat Train Sideways Boogie Shuffle Stomp'.

A working band on the road was one thing, it was part of the gig. But when one of the band members was literally a ticking time bomb, it was an odyssey that even the ever-patient Brown was regularly at wits' end as he chronicled in *Strange Brew.com*. "We tried hard. We made a record. We did lots of gigs. But Graham was damaged by his drug usage, so it was all very unpredictable."[106]

And it made for some choice memories as Brown ticked off in *White Rooms & Imaginary Westerns*. It was a seemingly never-ending series of drug, alcohol and mystical and rough character types orbiting Graham's non-stop dramas.

Throw in marital and relationship situations and it seemed that Bond & Brown were constantly on the brink of self-destructing. But, amazingly enough, the band managed to pull it together for the most part, thanks in no small part, to Brown's insistence that the music could keep the engine moving despite the constant threat of a Graham meltdown. By summer 1973, it looked like Bond & Brown might just survive Bond's antics and behaviour.[107]

Until suddenly the roof caved in on Brown's hopes and dreams.

Birmingham was a regular stop on the Bond & Brown tour itinerary which was good. What was bad was that Birmingham was like catnip for just about every vice and psychotic propensity in Bond's fevered mind. It became a ritual at every Birmingham gig for Bond, as chronicled by Brown "to be dragged off by a group of weird, occult professional types" and plied with alcohol, drugs and an ongoing array of dark mystical religious incantations.

Brown remembered in *Strange Brew.com* and *Record Collector.com* that Graham was damaged by his drug use (as well his growing interest in the dark arts). "By December 1973, Graham was going off the rails. Things went sour when Graham drank too much he became totally unreliable."[108]

Enter the straw that broke Bond & Brown. For good. The early portion of the group's final series of shows was immediately thrown into controversy when Bond's girlfriend, Diane, accused him of abusing her daughter which would be justified by Bond as part and parcel of his latest mystical beliefs. A few days later, with the band doing a show in Leicester, an old girlfriend of Bond's appeared out of nowhere and gave him some acid, which had an immediate negative effect. Although Brown and the band would give it their best shot, Bond played nothing but feedback, telling the crowd that it was he, in fact, who had invented feedback.

Brown did his best to stop Bond's downward spiral and, by association, the rest of the band who was suffering creatively and emotionally because of his antics. It all came to a head during a concert in Scarborough when, shortly after the set began, Bond unexpectedly collapsed and had to be rushed to a hospital.

Looking on in frustration, Brown determined that for him it was the last hurrah as he offered in *Record Collector.com*, *Strange Brew.com* and, with a definitive note of finality *White Rooms & Imaginary Westerns*. "If Graham was going to be so unreliable, I had to kick it all in the head. Towards the end of things, the drugs and other things got to be too much, and in the end I bailed. I had been on the road with hardly a break for the better part of five years. By the end of 1972, I was emotionally and physically drained. My life needed reappraising. It was also time for a proper holiday."[109]

# BROWN TAKES TIME OFF... NOT

One thing was certain. Anybody who could write songs for Cream, could quite easily qualify as a lyricist for good buddy Jack Bruce's 1972 second attempt at recreating the classic power trio with West Bruce & Laing. In conversation with this author, Brown was nonchalant when asked why he said where do I sign. "It was no mean feat," he said. I could always write hard rock songs."

Brown would look back on his West Bruce & Laing experience as mixed at best in *White Rooms & Imaginary Westerns*. He considered anytime with Bruce as time well spent. He did not think much of West and Laing as musicians, and he would ultimately fall prey to yet another songwriting hustle in which he received only a quarter of the songwriting royalties and it would take thirty-seven years to see a penny of it. "The band did well by most standards but they couldn't become the next Cream which was what everybody was hoping for. But Jack and I wrote some good stuff for them like 'Out In The Fields' and 'Like A Plate' (which was a song about blow jobs)."[110]

But it was safe to say that Brown was a bit distracted as he attempted to keep Bond & Brown on course and offers up an audible sigh as he looks back on the inevitability of it all with the author. "We were having some success but, in the end, the Graham situation wasn't going really well. We had both been low when we got together so we just got together and did it. We did an incredible amount in the year we were together. Unfortunately, Graham didn't know how to take care of himself."

By the time Bond & Brown had called it quits, Brown

had already returned to the creative womb of Jack Bruce with the album *Out Of The Storm*. And after half a dozen records and no small amount of creative and ego driven spats, it was work but, for Brown, it was all too familiar and, by degrees comfortable work.

When it came to the process between Bruce and Brown, it was easy and, more often than not, comfortable. Brown told the author why he continued to come back for more... "The relationship (with Bruce) was always up and down. Sometimes it was hard and sometimes it really pissed me off. Other times it was all sweetness and light. You're talking about two very large personalities. Sometimes it was just one too many. Jack was always very competitive and I am not like that."

Brown remained busy but in the short run following the demise of Bond & Brown, doing the occasional poetry reading and fitting in bits and pieces of holiday travel with his girlfriend Sue in places such as Tunisia, Sardinia and the Caribbean. But all the good times and alone time could not erase his time with Graham Bond and was leaving some mental scars as he confessed to the author. "I was still very upset with the way that whole Graham Bond thing ended, and I did take a step back and attempted a bit of a vacation."

But mentally, the idea of suddenly becoming a man of leisure was losing ground to the desire to, quite simply, be a working musician and do what working musicians do. "I was determined to carry on. I was determined with the idea of being in a band. I was determined that I could improve. I had been around a lot of great musicians and there was a lot going on with music and it all seemed to work for me."

Brown would be a musical Don Quixote throughout 1973. He reunited with several former members of the Bond & Brown band and recorded some demos which were unsuccessful in attracting label interest. He would also cross paths with a promising band called Ro Ro. Once again Brown recorded some demos with the group which, if nothing else, would allow him to keep his songwriting and producing chops. In the tradition of no-good deed going unpunished, Brown had the occasion to use Ro Ro as his backup band during a live performance that was attended by representatives of RSO Records. The ever-social Brown ended up introducing the members of Ro Ro to the RSO people who ended up signing a deal with RSO. As far as Brown fared with RSO, the label said thanks but no thanks.

To put things mildly, Brown seemed to be pissing into the wind. There was enough poetry reading gigs to keep his profile somewhat visible but ultimately it was taking him away from what had been a songwriting career in ascendency to being just a semi name again.

Brown played it cool in the face of his questionable luck. But he made it plain in conversation with the author that he was fighting a losing battle with his Jones Road. "I really couldn't get away from the road. I did feel at the time that I had a lot more to prove. I was a maverick. I was addicted to the road and doing gigs. I didn't want to stop."

Despite his dogged determination, word along the music/poetry hotline was that post Bond & Brown, Brown had hit an extremely hard luck dry spell with lots of promises and few successes and that Cream royalties and the money earned from the poetry readings was keeping him solvent. In the darkest corners, there was speculation that Brown, like most pop culture icons, had had his moment in the sun and was now fallen by the wayside.

But in Brown's world, the watch word remained 'never say never'.

David Apps, Brown's former agent during the short-lived Bond & Brown period and currently acting as Brown's manager, had stumbled upon a part-time gig as an A&R man with Decca Records progressive rock subsidiary Deram.

Brown liked the idea of looking for bands with potential and taking the most promising on via a publishing deal to Deram and get them deals.

Over the short haul, Brown would see a lot of acts, take the ones that seemed to him to have some kind of commercial potential to Deram which, for reasons too numerous to list but ultimately falling on the wrong side of money and prevailing commercial potential, passed on all of Brown's discoveries.

However, the free and easy nature at Deram would afford Brown the luxury of playing at producer in some offbeat sessions, one that brought a feeling of accomplishment as documented in a Facebook entry memory. "I made a single out of a song that Graham Bond and I had written for a documentary film about Malta called *Maltimour*. We had an all-star line-up for the session that included Jack Bruce on bass and, somehow, we got Jeff Beck to come down. He did three quick and totally miraculous passages on the solo section and some obligatos. Then he turned to me and said, 'I think you've got all you need there.' And after payment he left and, indeed, we had it."[111]

Around the same time, Brown got a chance to pay Beck back for his help with a lyrical contribution to Beck's attempt at the short-lived power trio concept which he also discussed on Facebook. "I got involved with Jeff's venture with Tim Bogert and Carmine Appice (Beck Bogert & Appice). I wrote a ballad for them and a rocker I had written with Jim Mullen called 'Living Life Backwards'."[112]

Creatively it would not be a total loss. While Decca did not have a clue as to what they should be signing in the early seventies, their imprint Deram saw much value in Brown and his poetry and signed Brown to record his poetry to a musical backing for a one-off album entitled *The "Not Forgotten" Association*.

Brown would take this recording as an opportunity to

revisit old times with long standing musicians Taff Williams, Ed Spevock, Jeff Clyne and Viv Stanshall providing the backing. Ever the realist, Brown acknowledged that the only reason *The "Not Forgotten" Association* was commissioned by Deram was to help fill out their catalogue. But he would get the satisfaction that what was essentially a throwaway for the label would sell really well and get some good reviews.

Deram would end up sending Brown out on a bit of a tour to promote *The "Not Forgotten" Association* which when coupled the latest round of poetry readings and the occasional odd side gig with some musician friends, would do wonders for Brown's wanderlust but would be the final nail in the coffin of his long-term relationship with Sue.

Brown is cautious, speaking haltingly when addressing the subject but, over the years, has been more than willing to address his ex on several occasions. In a 2010 remembrance that appeared in *White Rooms & Imaginary Westerns*, Brown reflected, "The writing was on the wall between Sue and me. My greed for new faces and new places had finally won."[113]

Ten years later and in conversation with this author, Brown was more circumspect. "Sue and I had been together for more than five years and I was still on the road quite a bit. Sue was getting into acting but she really wanted to settle down, get married and have a family. I wasn't ready for that. After Sue and I broke up, I went freelance when it came to women for a long time."

Still, Brown was not throwing up his hands at the prospect of being romantically unattached, not being the type to wallow in his loneliness. A lifeline would come his way in the guise of old friend Dickie Markstein who called in desperation to see if Brown was interested in playing percussion on a thirty-date tour. Brown recalled in *White Rooms & Imaginary Westerns*, that it didn't take long for him to say yes. "I didn't want to sit around in the ruins of my romance, I immediately said yes.

Having virtually no responsibility except to get up and play when required. I had a great time, using my freedom to make a lot of new friends."[114]

Another phone call from Jack Bruce would give Brown the opportunity to go to the United States for the first time as well as to play tourist and hangout with some of the big names in music and film, who at the time were doing enormous amounts of angel dust and, in the process, managing to create great art. Brown would be both amused and amazed at the luxury and debauchery of the experience as he flew back to England.

Upon his return he would be greeted by some tragic news. Brown would get an up close and personal look at the final damaged days of his good friend Graham Bond.

After the demise of Bond & Brown, Bond had fallen into rapid decline. At one point, Bond would proclaim he was now both drug and mysticism free and that from that point on he would devote himself completely to music and, particularly, jazz. Brown would take his good friend at his word and would step in on his behalf, approaching several record labels and finding some interest in giving Bond another chance.

Things seemed to be turning a corner. Bond had taken an apartment near Brown and communication between the two had improved. Then one day there was a knock on the door. Brown immediately expected the worst. Bond had unexpectedly disappeared, and nobody had seen or heard from him for a few days. Brown feared the worst when the caller turned out to be the police and, as he recalled in *White Rooms & Imaginary Westerns*, "The police rang to tell us that Graham had been killed by a tube train at *Finsbury Park Station*. It was never really established whether he jumped or was pushed."[115]

# PETE'S PREAMBLE TO DANCING WITH MR. D

Creativity and immortality. When you've lived the kind of life Pete Brown has lived, it's easy to see the correlation. Brown chose the occasion of the passing of Jack Bruce to creatively address the issue in poem. *What Is There Left To Say?* Was written as a dedication to Bruce. But Brown has lived a long life and substituting any of the musicians he has spent time and a life with would work under any circumstances.

**What is there left to say?**
What is there left to say?
When the last notes have died away
When the last leads have been disconnected
And the last fees have been collected
When the last dressing room's been deserted
And the last hurt's no longer hurting
And the last stage has been struck
And the last gears' un the truck
And the last notes have died away
What is there left to say?

# DANCING WITH MR. D

Mal Dean was a cartoonist, painter and illustrator who had created the covers for *A Meal You Can Shake Hands With In The Dark*, *Thousands On A Raft*, *The "Not Forgotten" Association* and *Things May Come And Things May Go, But The Art School Dance Goes On Forever*. He died on 24th February 1974, two months before his thirty-third birthday.

Less than three months later, Graham Bond died on 4th May. 1974 was not a good year for Pete Brown.

Brown had always been close to people and when they passed, it was often a melancholy reflection. The passing of Dean and Bond, mere months apart, struck a reflective tone in Brown. "The deaths of Graham Bond and Mal Dean left a big hole in my life, accompanied by a whole lot of guilt. Mal had been a close friend an important part of my support system and Graham had encouraged me to sing, without which my life would have been a lot less rich. I hadn't been around enough for Mal and felt that I had acted too late for Graham. I dreamed about them for a long time afterwards and I still find it hard to think that they are really gone, all these years later,"[116]

As with all life issues he faced, Brown dealt with the deaths of Dean and Graham by plunging into his work. Long hours of rehearsals on various projects. Including rehearsals for a memorial performance for Dean, and little or no sleep had become Brown's stock in trade in 1974. And not surprisingly, Brown pushed things over the edge. In all fairness, Brown seemed to have a sixth sense about testing his physical and psychological limits.

But they would have to go back to his traumatic LSD freakout in 1967 to come up with the equivalent of the nightmare he experienced in 1974 which he described in *White*

*Rooms & Imaginary Westerns.* "During rehearsals with The Flying Tigers band who I had discovered and was developing, I was also working with Jack (Bruce) a lot. At one point we worked all night and I slept for about an hour before returning to London and rehearsing. At the end of the rehearsal, we jammed for a while and then I went home. Wired from the combination of no sleep and adrenalin, I began to feel ill."[117]

But that did not prevent the self-proclaimed workaholic from jumping on anything he felt was worth his time. One short lived attempt at something was a relatively brief amalgamation called Brown And Friends. It was a loose group of Brown's friends and esteemed musicians that included Jack Bruce, Jeff Beck, Alan Ross, Tony Fernandez, Bob Jackson, and a host of others. They turned out some fairly interesting music over a series of demos but even with Bruce and Beck on board, record labels were not interested. The emotions had barely dried on this attempt at something by Brown then he was on to the next.

Brown was in a dangerous state.

Instinctively he knew something was wrong. Brown continued to reflect on those dark moments with the author. "I laid down on the bed and tried to rest, but seemed to be hovering two inches above it, unable to get out of the bed, I crawled across the road to a nearby doctor's office. He gave me a big yellow pill. But it didn't help. So I got a cab to a local emergency room hospital. I was seen by a doctor; told I had high blood pressure and to go home and try and relax."

Brown was not one to take relaxation lightly, point of fact, the songwriter seemed to be constantly fighting a losing battle, his health versus his creative drive. In desperation, and at the suggestion of Bruce, Brown went to see yet another physician.

Dr. Meg Peterson was quick and to the point. "She deduced quite rightly that I wasn't looking after myself. In her words, I was putting too much out and not putting enough back I had no reserves of strength. The remedy was exercise. To say the least, I was scared of making a fool of myself at a gym or jogging, so I elected to swim. I had never been taught properly so I confidently presented myself at the local pool, got in, did half a length and sank to the bottom."

Brown persisted and his improved athletic prowess would go a long way toward keeping his high blood pressure under control. Which was good because Brown was at his best when he was busy and into '74 and '75 he was nothing if not that, with work with Bruce always on the horizon and a wide assortment of spot gigs, poetry readings and what would turn out to be his prize possession of the moment The Flying Tigers, a group that afforded the opportunity to work with respected keyboard player/composes Ian Lynn.

Brown discovered the band on one of his many excursions, liked their spunk and spirit and felt he could do something with the band's progressive soul/jazz influences in the way of a label deal. So just like that, Brown was producer, songwriter and de facto manager to a band with a lot of potential. And as Brown knew, potential often needed a lot of work.

Brown soon had them working on demos and getting The Flying Tigers off and running. Brown enjoyed the challenge of piloting the fortunes of The Flying Tigers and would often find himself amused at the band's accident-prone nature.

The night before The Flying Tigers very first gig under Brown's guidance, the band's drummer, who celebrated a bit too hard and with too many joints, sleepwalked out of a fourth story window and slammed hard to the concrete below, surviving the fall but breaking his back in the process. Brown was faced with finding a replacement on zero notice but The Flying Tigers made the gig.

The snake bit nature of the band would continue on the very next gig when the band, not known for automotive skills, would essentially destroy three vehicles over the course of a 100-mile journey to the show. Fortunately, the gig was relocated at the last possible minute which allowed The Flying Tigers, through it all, to arrive on time.

Through it all, Brown still found himself in an emotional quandary. Sue and his relationship was all but non-existent at this point and Brown had long since resolved the 'relationship and exclusivity' issue by being footloose when it came to one night stands. But the pair had been together long enough to have a bond and so they agreed in 1975 to go on holiday together.

If the intent for this jaunt to Corfu was one last chance at romance, then by all accounts, their time together was a success. If it was a last gasp attempt at determining whether a true relationship was possible, then Corfu would be their last hurrah.

"It was a time of endings," Brown wistfully said in *White Rooms & Imaginary Westerns*. "Sue and I finally split, though we would remain good friends, even to this day."[118]

An even bigger professional disappointment would be Brown's seemingly doomed attempts at developing a band and bringing it home to riches and success for all concerned. The Flying Tigers had continued to be Brown's best effort in many a moon. They worked a lot, playing live and regularly at several London residency clubs and acquiring requisite positive reviews along the way. Some quite good.

The Flying Tiger demos were making the rounds of the record labels and would often result in record company reps in the audience at their gigs. They looked, they listened but, when it came down to matters of commerciality, what was hip at the moment on the charts and the final thumbs up or thumbs down by people who knew more about making money than making music, nobody bit.

The Flying Tigers would go down that inevitable road,

making money but not enough. Brown's kindred spirit in the band, Ian Lynn, saw the handwriting on the wall and left the band. The Flying Tigers would continue on for a bit but eventually dissolved. In hindsight, Brown blamed himself for the band's failure to click. "I think that my trying to manage people at the same time caused confusion," he said in *White Nights & Imaginary Westerns*. "I was never very convincing as a businessman. I belong on stage or in the studio."[119]

Deciding what his next step would be gave him the time to visit his parents Nat and Kitty. What he discovered, quite simply, was that his parents were aging rapidly and not for the best. Nat had had a heart attack at one point and had spent time in the hospital while Kitty was now suffering from diabetes. For Brown, reconnecting with his parents on any level was an emotional marathon. Tradition, reality, changing attitudes and the presence of immortality and end of life as his parents passed into their twilight years. It was something worth revisiting and considering but, for Brown, it was a step he was not yet ready to go down.

That's when Brown made the decision. "I decided to try my luck in New York," he recalled in *White Rooms & Imaginary Westerns*. "I wasn't ready or good enough to make this move, but I did it."[120]

Armed with a skeletal list of contacts, Brown made his way to New York where he immediately fell in love with the vibe of the city. It was exciting, pulsating, creatively alive. As he checked into a hotel in a hip part of town, he realised that the City That Never Sleeps was his kind of place. And in a sense it would be. Brown would meet hip business types and watch as legendary musicians strutted their stuff on stage. But when it came to striking out and making some hay in the business side, Brown was hearing all talk and no action. With one notable exception.

Stan Poses was a bit of an east coast muckety muck on the

business side, overtly friendly and more than willing to take him around town and introduce Brown to people. When he was not playing tour guide and gladhanding, he also worked for a high-profile management, publishing and production company who, with no small amount of largesse, offered Brown a new publishing deal. As his current publishing deal was about to run out, he was definitely interested. But he was also leery of contracts these days and so…

"I took the contract to a lawyer in a high-rise skyscraper to scrutinise," he said in *White Rooms & Imaginary Westerns*. "Before I was allowed in I had to pay $500. The lawyer took my money and looked at the contract for about three minutes. I asked him what he thought? He said, 'Put it this way, you'd be better off jumping through that window. I went home a few days later."[121]

# PETE CAN SING PETE HATES PUNK

Brown touched down back in the UK. He was right back where he started from. Which meant he was still looking for a gig. But at least now, he was going around in much better voice. There's a history of the Brown's having more than adequate pipes. But for the longest time, the Brown lineage of superior singers seemed to have stopped with Pete.

"My father had a great voice, a natural voice, which my daughter inherited," Brown offered in a *Music From The Head And Heart* conversation. "I had to work really hard at it."[122]

Encouragement for Brown to sing came from, of all places, Graham Bond during Brown's post Cream scuffling days. But it was the reality side of business, ergo you want a record deal all the best songs in the world won't mean much if you can't sing them, that, by 1966, pushed Brown, all talent aside, to enlist a music teacher to teach him the vocal ropes. It was no huge secret that Brown was learning how to sing in a proper rock and roll manner. But it was only in the mid-seventies, after more than a decade of proper instruction that Brown, stepped forward to announce that he could now actually sing for his supper.

"I had found a great teacher (Eve Johnson) and had been with her for six years," Brown told the author. "She was wonderful. She was very much from a classical/cabaret technique and for me that approach to singing proved very sustainable."

Brown would spend much of 1976 into '77 at a rather leisurely pace, doing the odd demo, knocking on a few doors looking for deals and doing a lot of just hanging out. Meanwhile the band Back To The Front, who many would consider promising — amazingly so considered what was evolving musically in the UK — were continuing to get gigs in places that were largely old school in attitude and who favoured superior musicians in a live setting. But there remained a sense of irony and frustration that a band that was uniformly so good could not get a record deal to save their lives.

Brown could sense a change in the wind. He could see what was in the clubs and what was being played on the radio and, perhaps most telling, who were getting deals. To his way of thinking, it was not a pleasant time for what he considered real music. And get Brown ranting on the state of late seventies music as a whole, as did *Strange Brew* and *All About Jazz.com* it must have been a fairly easy task.

"It was punk time in Britain," lamented Brown, "and what we were doing meant nothing at the time. When you look back on that period of time, it was a nightmare for British music because it was the first time the music business had invented something themselves rather than having discovered it. The result was that basically it damaged British music very badly. When the punk thing came along I was completely horrified by it and thought that was something that was destroying the skill base of British music. You couldn't get a record deal at the time because they just wanted people who couldn't play but who looked right. At the time, Back To The Front were doing reasonably well because so many people hated punk live. Unfortunately the punk thing was something that the record business invented and rammed down everybody's throat."[123]

Given his perfectionist nature, it was not surprising that as the wave of punk rock washed over the UK, Brown was quick to find the guilty party. "I thought I wasn't doing my job well enough. So I felt I'm just going to give up."[124]

In fact, the continued near misses only succeeded in

encouraging Brown to continue to actively seek any and all creative avenues. His continued mania for film and how it seemed to go hand in hand with the type of music he was making was whetting his imagination and that, maybe, his next step might be in some area of film. The Edinburgh Film Festival would prove to be a step in that direction. As a long-time friend of the festival producer, Linda Myles, Brown suddenly found himself in a different kind of creative universe, one populated by a different breed of creative minds.

For Brown, the highpoint or the festival would be his introduction to producer/director Martin Scorsese who was making the rounds with his latest film, *Alice Doesn't Live Here Anymore*. Brown was enthralled with the man, a quite intelligent mind to his thinking and, almost immediately, further turned Brown's mind to cinematic possibilities. "We seemed to get on very well," he recalled in *White Rooms & Imaginary Westerns*. "He was a big Cream fan and asked me to get in contact the next time I was in Los Angeles. The long-time film fanatic in me was beginning to think I might take a crack at screen writing. I had an idea."[125]

The cinematic courtship would continue for Brown as a subsequent trip to Los Angeles, hanging out with Scorsese and his cool friends and, perhaps the most enticing, the filmmaker's offer to introduce the by now wide-eyed songwriter to his producer and agent.

Brown continued to be susceptible, even as this latest fantasy stood out in lights in his psyche. Brown's mind, as always, was back on the road and, somehow, someway, he continued to want to get that party started and play music. "I was scared and unprepared for such a possibility," he reflected in *White Rooms & Imaginary Westerns*. "I should have grabbed it and stayed. But I wasn't ready to let go of the music. In fact, I never would be."[126]

# ONCE MORE INTO THE BREECH

To say that Brown was at a loose end into 1977 would be a bit of an understatement. He still had enough faith in the essentially defunct Back To The Front to work tirelessly to make that band still relevant. There was the occasional demo that, despite the comparative quality with Brown at the helm, went nowhere. There would also be the phone call from out of nowhere. And like clockwork, a familiar voice came a calling.

And this way would bring temptation for Brown. Temptation named Jack Bruce.

When it came to Bruce, Brown had him pegged at this point. He was in a seemingly never-ending battle between his own literary and, often cavalier, attitudes towards music and musicians, the result being that good reviews aside, he was never able to get over the commercial divide that marked him by his work with Cream and, as a solo artist with *Songs Of A Tailor*. On a personal front, Bruce was getting older and his health was more and more an issue.

Long story short, Brown knew the challenges that faced him when he agreed to write for the album *How's Tricks* and said yes anyway. The creative back and forth between Bruce and Brown was predictable. Brown wrote the lyrics, Bruce gave a thumbs up or down or made a pointed suggestion that Brown inevitably followed on the nine of the ten slices of blues, jazz and rock that featured *How's Tricks* as credited to The Jack Bruce Band. In hindsight Brown saw the album as decidedly understated. But as he recalled in *White Rooms & Imaginary Westerns*, there were issues that centred on both Bruce and RSO Records.

"Sadly, there were problems. The record label failed to

distribute *How's Tricks* with the tour that followed and, for my opinion, the obvious single, 'Something To Live For', was vetoed. Could this have had something to do with the fact that Tony (Hymas) and I wrote it?"[127]

Speculation aside, *How's Tricks* would not be the smash hit everybody was hoping for, topping off at a meagre 153 on the *Billboard* charts and furthered the widening chasm between RSO and Bruce. But at the end of the day it was just business and contracts and the upshot was that Bruce was still on the hook to RSO and so, less than a year later, Brown would contribute to an admittedly half-hearted album entitled *Jet Set Jewel*.

The album, ten tracks of various soul/jazz/rock elements and featuring Brown lyrics on five songs, was the final nail in the coffin. RSO would reject the album outright as being blatantly uncommercial (although the album would finally be released in 2003 on Polydor Records) and, shortly thereafter, would drop Bruce from the label. Brown thought that would be it, at least for the time being, for his association with Bruce.

But when it came to the creative life of Brown and Bruce, one could never truly say never. And when Bruce rang up Brown for a one song lyrical contribution to the album *I've Always Wanted To Do This*, a literal busman's holiday of jazz/pop art fusion featuring Bruce and friends Clem Clempson, Billy Cobham and David Sancious, it all sounded too progressive to pass up.

Brown's contribution to the song *In The Way* was too good. Outside of the fact that Epic Records, Bruce's last major label for nearly a decade, would ultimately die as a commercial death, it gave Bruce and company the chance to take the album's music on the road and to showcase great musicians doing what they do best, which is to play.

Despite being literally on call for Bruce between 1977-1980, Brown had plenty of free time to explore other musical possibilities. After a couple of false starts with, essentially, pick up bands, Brown and good friend Ian Lynn got serious enough to solidify a new round of attempts to make Back To The Front into something.

On the surface, the band seemed to have it all. They would gig regularly, playing a heady concoction of jazz/blues/soul and a bit of funk for good measure. For Brown, the chemistry of Back To The Front was potent and a return to traditional road/performing vibe that worked for him on a soulful level.

Back To The Front had a fairly short but lucrative run but it was nothing if not eventful. During one gig, the drummer had a brain freeze and forgot what he was supposed to be playing. On a personal note, Brown, who was just coming into his own as a front man and newly minted singer of some skills, lost his voice which required a trip to a doctor whose borderline medieval treatment of probing skewers down his throat and huge lozenges surprisingly did the trick. But at the end of the day, Brown, as well as the rest of the band, knew there was no way in hell Back To The Front would ever get a record deal.

And Brown was very much the realist in ticking off the reason why in *White Rooms & Imaginary Westerns*. "We were too old. We were too jazz like. We were too out of date. We were too far ahead. You name it, we weren't it."[128]

But Brown had always been a restless spirit, fully capable of knowing when a venture had run its course and equally adept to jumping to any number of Plan Bs already mentally filed away for future reference. When the epitaph was finally written on Back To The Front in 1978, Brown quickly jumped into an all-star charity gig alongside such top flight musicians as Dick Heckstall-Smith and Mitch Mitchell.

It was also during this period that he made the acquaintance of Phil Ryan, late of the noted band Man and a couple of, if you blinked you missed them, solo albums. Brown and Ryan immediately found that they got along in a blues soul sort of vibe and would go on to collaborate.

Suddenly free of all professional and personal encumbrances, Brown found himself on a rollercoaster ride between England and Los Angeles, where he mixed and mingled with countless people in the music and film industry and picked up the odd gig along the way and, most importantly to his way of thinking, yet another publishing deal with Intersong Music. As always, with Brown, hope was always eternal and just around the corner.

Throughout the spring and summer of 1979, there was a blur of activity. Brown and Ryan were constantly in the studios, demoing songs. Brown would have his creative mettle tested when the opportunity arose to write lyrics to the music of Thelonious Monk for singer Robert Wyatt but the project was ultimately cancelled.

1979 would end on a dire note. Brown's father, Nathan's, health was deteriorating rapidly. In a matter of months, bouts of jaundice and heart issues had transformed into a diagnosis of cancer. By the end of September, Nathan was admitted to the hospital where large doses of painkillers plunged him into endless bad dreams and hallucinations. Brown remained constantly on vigil as he expected his father's last days to tick. On *Yom Kippur*, The Jewish Day Of Atonement, Brown's father passed away.

"Eventually we got the call that he was losing it," Brown painfully recalled in *White Rooms & Imaginary Westerns*. "But when we arrived at the hospital, he was already gone. When confronted by the lifeless body, Kitty tried to reason with the doctors, as if a spare part, however expensive, might be found somewhere to bring Nathan back to life."[129]

# THE EIGHTIES...
# AS IN USELESS

Brown being a man of words and all, it was not surprising that he would be quick on the literary trigger. The eighties? In a word useless.

But when pressed by this author, Brown could be a bit more specific. "When the whole punk thing came about, I was pretty disgusted with it. I didn't want any part of it. The film thing was what I was about. After all, I was always a kind of a buff. Nothing really came of it but I was working. I still had my things with bands and poetry readings. I was doing okay."

Martin Scorsese would develop into Brown's emotional mentor by the start of the decade, always encouraging him to give screenwriting a go. Brown took what he considered a risky step in that direction when he presented the director with an idea for a rock and roll coming of age story set in the sixties entitled *Railhouse Jock And His Way To The Stars*. Scorsese would be enthusiastic and encouraging about the idea.

Brown set about writing the script and, and in the way of testing the waters on his screenwriting prospects, joined up with a workshop/advocacy group called The Association Of Independent Producers. At one of those workshops, *Railhouse Jock And His Way To The Stars*, had its official unveiling which so impressed BBC Producer Ken Todd who promptly commissioned the script for production with the BBC's *Play For Today* series.

Just like that Brown was awarded a commission of £1,800 for the script. Brown could not believe it was that easy. He was now a professional screenwriter. And just like that, Brown discovered the reality of a British film industry that was nothing if not in decline and was notorious for paying out on scripts that would ultimately never get made.

But Brown was not discouraged. "I just started writing film scripts," he said in a *Strange Brew.com* interview. "I actually got a very good literary agent and he got me a lot of work. But a lot of the things I wrote never got made. I think they were a bit idiosyncratic."[130]

But there would be the occasional bright spot to highlight his script writing adventures. Easily one of his more obscure credits would be a script entitled *Felix The Movie* which found a home with an American production company and would, over the years, air on various movie and television outlets, most notably The Disney Channel.

Brown ruefully recalled that his best intent for the film was that it was made and released. But in typical Hollywood fashion, too many money people got their hands in and spoiled the cinematic broth.

Also of note was Brown's gig, writing the dramatic links to a Rolling Stones documentary film entitled *Rewind*. It was a quick and relatively easy one day gig for which Brown received £1,000. Sadly, he had not cut himself in for any residuals and *Rewind* proved quite successful, Brown would get nothing more. During this period, Brown and good buddy Phil Ryan also managed to get a song into the soundtrack of a film/book called *Red Shift*.

*Red Shift* would be the official unveiling of Brown and Ryan but the reality was that the two musicians had long been compatriots of a kind and, right up there with Jack Bruce and Graham Bond, Phil Ryan may well have been one of the most important musical influences Brown would cultivate.

In a rough and ragged sort of way, Brown and Ryan were the classic example of opposites attracting according to Brown in *Strange Brew.com*. "Phil and I were both pretty strong left wingers. We used to fight a lot because even though I came from a working-class background, at the point where we started working together, I was relatively wealthy."[131]

Ryan and Brown would cross paths quite a bit in the day. Ryan was in a band called Eyes Of Blue which played the club circuit regularly and, when Brown wasn't on the hunt for women, he would hear Eyes Of Blue and, when it came to Ryan, he liked what he heard.

The pair got together musically for a time, wrote a couple of songs together that never went anywhere. But they stayed active and in touch and when Eyes Of Blue folded a slot opened up in what would be the second incarnation of Piblokto. Brown snapped Ryan up to join what would be a musically productive couple of years for both Piblokto and the two musicians.

"Phil joined the band Man and I ended up playing percussion on a couple of Man albums," he told *Strange Brew.com*. "It was around that time that I realised that, ever since Back To The Front had broken up, what I really needed in my life was Phil in order to write the things that I wanted to write, the more personal and idiosyncratic things and so we got together and started making demos."[132]

In relatively short order, the demos morphed into a full-blown band situation going under the moniker of The Interoceters. The band was made up of seasoned veterans, the compositions were first rate. Brown was high on the project and, as he had done so many times in the past, he began making the rounds of the record labels. Not totally unexpected was that the record companies, for various reasons, said thanks but no thanks. But Brown had become quite the expert in playing the label rejection game and was not deterred and pushed on.

While he pursued the music and the inevitable challenges, Brown was having some fun dabbling in the movie world. Film people, to his way of thinking were very much like musicians, wildly creative and just as wildly unpredictable. Being around film people was a welcome respite from the bad taste that the onset of punk had left in Brown's soul. So while he would occasionally plug away at a script for the bucks and the yucks, Brown would find that throughout the early to mid-eighties, the music would continue to call him back.

To what, at best would be considered a classic, surreal look at the Brown hustle, often humorous, ironic and never boring. More on a lark than anything else, Brown and his writing buddy Ryan cobbled together a bizarre bit of business called 'Don't Take Your Fish To The Swimming Pool'. About a man who loses his woman at a swimming pool and resorts to the company of inflatables to sooth his sadness. The intent on Brown's part was to get the song to 'way out there' jazz great Eddie Harris. Harris eventually received the song but ultimately passed on the grounds that he felt that the song was too weird.

Yet another stab at managing almost bore fruit until Brown looked at the final contract drawn up by his management which was horribly weighed in his favour but not his clients. Brown's sense of fairness cut to the quick and the result was that a contract that would have favoured him at the expense of his own client fell through.

In the early eighties, Brown, looking to reconnect with his fellow Piblokto bandmate, Ian Lynn, Brown and Lynn collaborated on a one of bit of prog rock business called Party In The Rain, a raw and very smart bit of business that would do quite well internationally.

The advantage of playing in several different playgrounds produced several moments of geeking out as well as madness and disappointment. On one trip to Los Angeles, Brown found himself in the presence of legendary B movie filmmaker Roger Corman, the creator of such classics in questionable taste as *The Raven* and *A Bucket Of Blood*.

On another business outing, he would run into one of his all-time favourite science fiction writers, Robert Sheckley who offered him a gig adapting some of his stories for an upcoming project. Brown would be all for it until the money for the project, in typical Hollywood fashion, fell through. Along the way, there would be several bouts of ill-fated attempts at romance and/or lust.

Mid way through the eighties, Brown would concede that, while he was getting work and paying the bills, nothing was really touching his desires professionally or personally. "I was totally adrift," he offered in *White Rooms & Imaginary Westerns*. "The writing jobs were frequent, but they were rarely leading to anything positive. 1985 was the absolute worst year for gigs. The only thing I remember doing that year was a charity show with Mick Jagger's brother Chris."[133]

1980-1985. For Brown, things could only get better.

# THINGS GET BETTER

And midway through the 1980s, they most certainly did. Amour came a knocking after decades of dalliances and false emotional alarms. Call it what you will, Brown was suddenly bit and it seemed like the real thing. True to his crisp and to the point nature, Brown got right to the business of explaining to the author in 2022 how it all happened. Watch out for details.

"I was working at a studio and, one day, the producer I was working with told me of this great little eating place around the corner and there was this waitress. I started going there pretty regularly."

"After a while she moved on to another restaurant around the corner which I liked even more. So I used to go there very regularly and by this time we had started chatting. One day I was walking down the street and I was in a really bad mood, and she (the waitress Sheridan MacDonald) was walking toward me from the other direction. I didn't acknowledge her because I was in such a bad mood. So I went to the restaurant where she worked and apologised for ignoring her. She said, 'Okay I'm moving to another place' and I said 'Okay, I'll see you around'."

"So, I went there one day for lunch and I looked at her and thought 'There she is, my wife to be.' There was definitely a mutual attraction. It started out fairly superficial, then we went together for a while, lived together for a long while and eventually we would get married. By that time I was okay with it."[134]

Succinct and to the point, no frills. This is how Brown saw it looking backward on one of the most important moments in his life and from a point of view that was borderline detached, ho-hum.

Flash back to 2010 and an entry in *White Rooms & Imaginary Westerns*. Love was a completely different animal. It was of the moment, of the now. You want details. Here's your details.

Brown began noticing Sheridan in the Café Brasserie and the Pasta Underground. "She had a soft Scottish voice and a rare kind of beauty."[135] The rudeness to Sheridan was, for you completist, the result of a blow up with a bank manager. She had a two-year-old son named Tad. She was about to take a trip to America. When she got back she would be working at a place called The Rotisserie. He went to lunch at The Rotisserie and asked her out.

The chemistry between them was good. Brown struggled with his feelings. Sheridan continued to live an independent lifestyle in the face of his emotional jealousy. "Finally, I admitted my jealousy to her and she asked me to make a choice. Swallowing my fear I made it. We have been together ever since."[136]

And now you have the whole story.

# SLOW AND EASY
# 1985 TO 1990

Nobody can say for certain that Brown, come hell or high water, ever said no to a gig. But into the eighties, when Brown was offered the opportunity to go to Paris to work as a producer and translator for a rising pop star named Laurent Voulzy, he found himself on the horns of a personal dilemma. His mother, Kitty's diabetes had worsened and she had been hospitalised. Brown wanted to go to Paris but his loyalty to family was on the verge of him cancelling the gig.

Brown would waver for days before the doctor's assurance that she had been stabilised tipped his decision in favour of going to Paris and the gig. Brown was having a good time in Paris and the gig was fairly well paid but his mind was constantly on his mother's condition. While in Paris, Brown was notified that his mother had passed He returned home, arranged for Kitty's funeral and set about sorting out a number of issues.

His relationship with Sheridan was still in the early, sorting it out stage and so Brown was dealing with a degree of stress and unrequited temptation on that front. Professionally, things for Brown were slow. Very slow. Brown would often state that the only performing gig he had in 1986 was as part of a performance by the organisation Jazz Against Apartheid. Fortunately things would begin to pick up the following year.

A poetry gig with Mike Horovitz which featured the debut public performance of Brown playing drums. A gig with a pickup band in Putney. A poetry reading for the BBC series *Overseas At Bush House* and, on the truly exotic front, playing congas as the opening act for the poet/sculptor Liliane Lijn. All keeping Brown busy and pointing him in the direction of the next big challenge.

Which, in 1987, would result in the release of a fairly massive twenty-one-track compilation album entitled *Before Singing Lessons 1969-1977*, a perceived, in many corners, send up of the fact that Brown had spent several years, primarily in The Battered Ornaments and Piblokto, of the public ridicule he often received for his mediocre singing skills. Brown most likely had a last laugh as the album would go on to sell reasonably well.

The ever-persistent Brown would continue to butt heads with the film industry and would occasionally get a nibble. A potentially big bite came in the offer to write the script for a film biography on rock star and Brown's good friend Alex Harvey. Brown enthusiastically jumped into the project and, over the life of the project, would pull together more than forty hours worth of research on his life and times. It appeared to be a goer until a falling out between the shared production companies, Yorkshire TV and London International, over choice of director and the logistics of the project which ultimately went nowhere.

It was about that time that Jack Bruce came a calling with what had become an almost annual event. Bruce is going into the studio for a new album and Bruce needs Brown's help. For his part, Brown had already come to the conclusion that this album, *A Question Of Time*, would be an odyssey of creative frustration and moments of brilliance. Bruce being Bruce, Brown winced at what the acceptance would entail. But he still said he would be right over.

In hindsight, Brown, who would supply the lyrics to eight of the album's twelve cuts, considered *A Question Of Time* one of Bruce's best albums. Also looking back on the process, Bruce was Bruce which meant that Brown often saw his lifelong partner as insufferable and contrary to the point of madness. "I put a considerable amount of effort into it (the album), he related in *White Rooms & Imaginary Westerns*. "After the initial writing sessions, I went to the studio in San Francisco to finish the writing and to add any last-minute modifications. As before, there were contradictory attitudes from Jack. Some of the time we got on well, socially, and perhaps he was glad to have me around. Other times he seemed to feel that I was a strain on the budget. I wasn't happy when I went home though I continued to polish the lyrics from a distance. As it turned out, it was this record that was to cause a serious deterioration in our friendship."[212]

But as the eighties shuffled toward its inevitable conclusion, Brown, despite the constant love/hate relationship with Bruce, was in an upbeat mood. His relationship with Sheridan was beginning to solidify into some semblance of domestic bliss.

A successful commission in the cinema world resulted in Brown writing a musical jazz drama set during war time in the forties and the rebellious actions of a group of music loving French teens. This was definitely Brown's wheelhouse and the result was an entertaining bit of business that, to Brown's way of thinking, was a success, for the most part because it actually got made and out to the masses.

But it was when Brown's fortunes were definitely on the rise that the ugly side of Jack Bruce once again emerged to test Brown's intestinal fortitude. To Brown's way of thinking, business dealings with Bruce was always a minefield that Brown, who in these situations seemed to run headlong into what would almost certainly be chaos.

The latest stop on Bruce's highway to hell would be a nasty bit of business surrounding *A Question Of Time* as he would recall in detail in *White Rooms & Imaginary Westerns*.

"I shouldn't have got so angry when he handed me a large cheque over dinner for my publishing on *A Question Of Time*. But the piece of paper he gave me with the cheque stated no percentages (royalties) and included a commission for his manager. Nor did it state what part of the advance I was supposed to be getting. I hadn't been consulted on anything or been allowed to bring my manager or lawyer into the equation. It was just assumed that I would roll over. I gave him the cheque back."

But that would not be the end of it. Brown was pissed off at the shabby treatment and decided it was time to bring up managerial firepower. "There was a very ugly scene," he chronicled in *White Rooms & Imaginary Westerns*. "Jack was being evasive and shifty. It was a side of him that I had rarely witnessed. We sorted it out... But it resulted in total silence between us for nearly four years."[137]

However, Brown is quick to point out that the up and down events of the eighties had darkened his spirit and, in a reflective conversation with the author, he was alternately positive and excited about what the just concluded decade had brought and what the nineties portended in his life and beyond.

"We had our music and our bands, and I liked working in films even though not a lot happened with the scripts. The records we did, especially the things I did with Phil, were, for the most part, quite good even though they weren't huge critical or commercial successes. We put an awful lot of stuff into them, and it was stuff that I don't think anybody else has attempted in quite some time."

About to enter the nineties and about to turn fifty, Brown remained a dynamo who is not about to push pause on his life. Creatively and professionally, he remained on overdrive and is quick to rattle off a laundry list of projects in the works to prove his point. Slow down? Brown has a good-natured laugh at the notion that the phrase 'stop working' is in his vocabulary. "I don't want to stop working. Being a writer there's always something to do and I keep running into interesting stuff and interesting people to work with. I like to encourage people, especially the younger generation. And from their point of view, they look at me and it's a respect thing."

# IT AIN'T EASY: REFLECTION ON NATHAN AND KITTY

Pete Brown was A-1 for the most part when it came to being a good son. He was good about cleaning up after himself growing up. He'd come by for regular visits when he was older and out of the house. He was as Jewish as one could be in those hectic World War II days which was like his parents, often on the inconsistent side.

But in looking back with the author on the passing of his parents, Nathan and Kitty he made it clear that he would not play by the rules when they tried to ram a traditional/stable life down his throat just as he was discovering his passion, which was being a Beat/Bohemian/Poet, Jazz lover/ songwriter and all manner of very unorthodox lifestyle choices. "But I made peace with my parents and what they felt I should be doing with my life. It's a shame that they didn't understand me."

In their defence, Brown acknowledged that his parents were brought up in a much stricter, traditional world and, post-World War II, that world began and ended with making the rent. "They never understood what I did or what I was into. My parents were people who traded in cash. They made enough to get by. They sold shoes. They made enough to get by. They never got rich or had big shops. They had a place in the marketplace and kept at it for the last thirty years of their lives. It was hard for them to understand what I was doing and why I loved it so much."

As if to prove how entrenched their thinking was, he recalled "One time I took them this enormous cheque I had just received, and they thought I had forged it. They didn't understand things like royalties. It was tough being in a family that was just not getting it. To their way of thinking, they wanted me to be an accountant and a lawyer and to make lots of money. Being into things like poetry and jazz was something that was too alien to them."

# PETE HAS A NINETIES MOVEMENT

Going into the nineties, Brown was seemingly at peace and settled in both his personal and professional life. His relationship with Sheridan was becoming more committed and permanent. Professionally, he was not on the road as much as he was used to which left him work time for the welcome, often more cerebral writing and producing.

But anybody who knew Brown knew that the challenge that would set him off had to be somewhere on the horizon. And early in 1990, he would take a hint and find his windmill to tilt at. Brown continued to find stumbling blocks to a label for the music he had created with Phil Ryan, inevitably hearing the same litany of corporate excuses that all led to rejection. However, in the late eighties/early nineties, he recalled receiving a very sage bit of advice from a wise old hand at the distribution end of the business who essentially told Brown the facts of life in the music business entering the nineties.

Record labels were dealing with the financial implications of the financial fallout from the punk craze and the advent of the CD as the hip and cheap new way of getting more mileage out of existing music. Consequently, there was no real incentive to sign anything new and risky. Brown got that. But what he did not realise was that distributors at the other end of the pipeline were much more accepting of new label product. The advice to Brown was simple, form his own label, begin to think more in line of being a producer and ship his albums to distributors.

And so was born Interoceter Records. And true to form, Brown and Ryan's album, *Ardours Of The Lost Rake*, by

1991, was successfully manoeuvring its way through a maze of distribution deals and was out in the world. In the spirit of striking while the iron was hot, Brown, over the next two years, would plunge headlong into producing new music for distributors and the great white wonder that was the international market. Next out of The Interoceter label was an album entitled *Woza Nasu* by long-time friend Dick Heckstall-Smith.

Brown was coming around to the idea that making music was also a business. *Woza Nasu* was made on a fairly low budget in London, with a first-rate band and questionable accommodations. In the spirit of nostalgia, Brown would step out from behind his producer's hat long enough to add a bit of percussion to some cuts.

When not working non-stop, Brown would make occasional trips to Paris where a job had taken Sheridan for visits and brief holidays. Brown had reached a point in his relationship that he was convinced that it was going to work and Sheridan, had likewise, come to the conclusion that somehow, someway, this was all going to work.

A follow up to *Ardours Of The Lost Rake*, *Coals To Jerusalem* with Ryan and himself, was already in the completion stage well into 1991 and was primed for release along with Smith's *Woza Nasu*. Brown was warming to the idea of having his own label and getting the music out there. By 1992 it was all good in Brown's world.

# HIT THE ROAD PETE

Brown was as settled and as close to being a homebody as he had been in decades. Professionally he was growing accustomed to this producer/record label gig. More often than not he was figuratively and literally speaking close to home when it came to recording demos and albums and writing scripts. Perhaps most evident in 1992 was the fact that Brown and Sheridan seem to be making mental and emotional plans for being together in more than just the biblical sense.

Sheridan was tiring of work that was constantly taking her long distances from Brown to jobs she was more and more dissatisfied with. During one particular heart to heart, Brown asked her what she would rather be doing. Without hesitation, Sheridan said she had always wanted to be an actress. Brown would help the cause with tuition money for classes and, as she progressed, a number of small roles.

Sheridan's coming of age would be when Jon Morrison, a director friend of Phil Ryan was directing an off-West End production when the lead actress had to drop out. When Morrison suggested that Sheridan might like to give the role a try, she was more than a bit uneasy at the prospect. But she was determined, studied hard, did the play and received excellent reviews. Which would keep her in London and close to Brown.

Brown is fully aware that to tell the whole story is to venture into his private life and he seems perfectly at ease when the subject of his now wife Sheridan is broached by this author. And quite meticulous in talking about it. He starts with getting the dates right, which he estimates was in the period 1988-1990. "Things were going well for us and I believe that's when my life began to change. We had been together for a while but she was still living on her own. I was living in a flat for a while but then I bought this old derelict of a house and would have a lot of work done on it. When we decided things were getting serious, she moved into the flat with me and then we moved into the house."

But like all good, bad or indifferent relationships, Brown acknowledged to this author that there was more than simply crossing the threshold together. "When we first met, there were some differences that we had to work on. Sheridan had a kid and to a large degree, I was pretty much set In my ways. So there was a feeling out process. But as things got more serious and we decided we were going to live together. So, we lived together. We loved each other and, at that point, we decided that we were going to make this work. Obviously, at that point, neither one of us knew what the outcome of this was going to be."

It was ironic for the couple and the relationship in that about the time circumstances were bringing their lives close together, the fates were conspiring to put Brown back on the road at odd times. Brown attempted to make sense of his place in the nineties in conversation with the author. And one thing you become aware of when talking to Brown, he's fond of dropping lists of gigs, sessions and just about anything he's done or is doing. And he will be the first to admit that his habit of listing is equal parts ego and pride.

Brown turned a one-off demo session with up and coming pianist Mervyn Afrika and ended up being the token white guy in a one off gig with Afrika and his band. He joined 200 Fingers, a big band fusion outfit for a time, whose motto was no one gets fired from the band. He produced The Modesir Brothers, a complex bit of business which had Brown contemplating the possibilities of 4/4 time, struck a nostalgic bit of business by producing a band he knew from the seventies called Cold River Lady and did a session with Richard Sinclair, a long-time mate and a former member of a favourite band, *Caravan*.

"I'm not really sure what happened," Brown sheepishly said to the author about the sudden bounce in early nineties activity. "All I know is that I started doing a lot of production. I was working with people who liked what I was doing and I was getting a lot of stuff to do."

However, Brown is nothing if not a realist. He acknowledged to this author that a significant bit of his success circa 1990-1992 was the fact that his singing had improved to, in most cases, acceptable levels. But the realist in Brown also knew that while he was at his peak. He was also falling short of the mark. "It was good and it went on for a long time. But commercially, it didn't make any sense and it never did. I was never going to get rich but, creatively, I could sleep at night. I loved what I was doing, the live/performing thing was always a labour of love for me. I'd always been incredibly into that aspect of what I was doing. It defined my personality."

Following a bad bit of business with an attack of gout, Brown fully recovered and was once again off and running. In short order, he was back in the studio, recording demos for a jazz folk band called The Grown Ups and another band called Heaven On Wednesday. Sadly both bands, although quite good in Brown's estimation did not land a deal.

It was around that time that Brown landed his first American production deal for a blues rock band called Sunset Heights. If Brown was expecting this to be a sedate bit of business. He would discover that Sunset Heights had a bit of Graham Bond in them and it resulted in him taking a literal trip to the wild side that was full of band members with thuggish nature, alcohol, drugs, guns and various bad parts of US towns. Through it all, Brown managed to pull together a fairly decent album that was glaringly marred by mediocre bass playing. Consequently, no deal for Sunset Heights was in the offing.

Brown would once again return to the stage, reuniting

for a one-off gig with 200 Fingers that once again whet his appetite for the live life. So much so that, on the occasion of the release of the album *Coals To Jerusalem*, Phil Ryan and Brown resurrected The Interoceters band for what would be a quite successful twenty-six-date tour in support of the album.

Brown was in a decidedly up mood on where his professional and personal lives were going. So magnanimous in fact that he barely blinked an eye when he got a call from Jack Bruce, once again asking for help. Bruce's request would be more of an invitation. It seemed that Bruce had struck a deal with *Rockpalast*, the WDR TV programme in Germany, for a show that would celebrate his 50th birthday. An all-star line-up would include Ginger Baker, Clem Clempson, Gary Moore and, as an extra added inducement to Brown, the opportunity to sing some great songs. And, after several years of not speaking, Brown looked at the offer as a way to mend fences.

Chatting with Baker during rehearsals had a good vibe right up to the point where he went vintage Ginger and scared the hell out of the promoters. The show itself seemed to go quite well. Brown was well versed in the song list and had become quite good when it came to harmonies. At one point in the birthday/ made for TV event, Bruce and Brown laid down a quite good rendition of 'Politician' Everything seemed too good to be true on the vibe. As Brown would recall in *White Rooms & Imaginary Westerns*.

"At one point Jack came up and asked me, without a sense of irony, to shorten my contribution as I was singing too well. Considering our history, I ended up feeling totally underused on the show. It did, however, promote a bit of a thaw between Jack and myself which was welcome as we hadn't communicated for some time."[138]

# WHAT IF...
# THAW REVISITED

What if? That is the question. The child of speculation and reality. And if anybody is qualified to play the what if? game it's Pete Brown. So when the author put this to him, there was a definite pregnant pause.

What if there had not been that fateful call to his flat? What if there had not been a band named Cream who was looking for a lyrical helping hand? What if Pete Brown and Jack Bruce had not become creative cohorts?

Brown has heard variations on the Jack question for years. Just about every interview and feature has touched on the Brown/Bruce relationship in one form or another. His replies can be pat or, as on this occasion, thoughtful. "It's hard to say. I suppose if I hadn't gotten with Cream and Jack, and hadn't have made a little bit of money, it would have made me think about other things. I probably would have continued to do the poetry thing. That would not have been the worst thing in the world because I love doing the poetry. I don't know. I might have been more obscure, or I might have been more famous. I was scared of doing the music, but I always wanted to do it. That phone call to come by the studio and meet Jack gave me the answer."

And through years of songwriting, with Cream and nearly a dozen solo Bruce albums later, Bruce and Brown remained one of the most productive and, yes, unlikely of songwriting duos, full of frustrations, ego, and as witness the birthday incident, one in which Brown would serve as often as whipping boy as vital creative partner.

Brown addressed all the conflicts and contrary issues of their relationship by throwing up his hands. "Were we joined at the hip? Of course. Forty-eight years speaks for itself. Sometimes it went smoothly and sometimes it was a battle of two big egos in the room. Sometimes the things we were trying to do just didn't work. And sometimes they did."

And sometimes, when things got too heated creatively and personally, Brown admitted that the only recourse was to run the other way. "Yeah, we had a bit of a falling out over the years. He could be a bit of an asshole to me, but I never said that to Jack in so many words. There were times when being around Jack wasn't particularly good for my head. Some of the issues we had with some of his later solo albums were hard. I didn't really love myself for doing them. There were a couple of times when I just had to step away from Jack for long periods of time."

After one such protracted time apart, some years later, when yet another call from Bruce would put the defining nature of their relationship into perspective. "The album *Silver Rails* absolutely brought us full circle. At that point in time everybody knew that Jack had been ill for quite a while and that he was not going to be around much longer. One day, he called me up and said 'Look, I'm going to do a new record and I'd like you to partner with me on it. I knew he was not going to be around much longer, so I said, 'Okay. Of course.' A lot of things would be involved in making what Jack would call his 'old man' record. Obviously, there was a lot of emotion involved, there was the creative back and forth between us and we worked very hard on it. And I think that *Silver Rails* came out incredibly well."

# ONE SATISFIED CAT

Things were happening going into the second half of the nineties. And by Brown's journeyman standards, the things were all good.

His name was continuing to get around as somebody who was not only professional, music smart and adaptable to just about any situation but, in a business sense, could bring projects in on deadline and on budget. It also did not hurt that the always cycling nature of the music business and popular tastes had by the mid-nineties swung back around to find favour in blues and jazz — Brown's music of choice. Consequently, Brown was ready, willing and able to jump on the pony and ride.

"You have to keep going and I'm grateful to get the gigs," he reflected in conversation with the author. "Finances have gotten better. It's still up and down but I've got a nice house and an incredible tax bill. So, I must be doing something right."

Easily, the most satisfying gig of the period would be to produce a star-studded tribute to guitarist Peter Green, the legendary musician/songwriter of Fleetwood Mac's earthier blues period before going commercial. *Rattlesnake Guitar* would be a bit of an undertaking, recorded in studios in both England and the United States. Brown would be quick on the trigger with the research that produced a boatload of great music from his Fleetwood Mac and post Mac periods. There was a lot to do, and Brown was up for the challenge.

Fortunately, there would be a lot of old British musicians and mates who were more than happy to climb aboard for the project. The song 'Green Manalishi' would have the benefit of an appropriately creepy turn by Arthur Brown. Another high point for Brown would be the song 'Baby When The Sun

Goes Down' which received a vigorous workout by the duo of Southside Johnny and Foghat's Rod Price. On an emotional level, Brown would be choked up when the, by that time, a very sick, legendary guitarist Rory Gallagher came in the studio for what would be his very last recording session.

*Rattlesnake Guitar* would go out as a massive two record set and would do quite well internationally which, for Brown, would necessitate a promotional trip to Germany. Brown could get used to this producing stuff. But the realist in him realised that it would not always be smooth sailing as he would recall in *White Rooms & Imaginary Westerns*.

"I didn't realise that sooner or later you have to work with someone with whom you have no chemistry and just doesn't like your face. It happened with the next record I did, and it was a shock."[139]

A deal for guitarist Innes Sibun, fresh off a stint with Robert Plant, was struck and the two decamped to the studio for what was to be blues and soul and that's where things got a bit dicey. Brown, ever the historian when it came to traditional music, would attempt to get through to Sibun regarding the subtleties of what they were trying to accomplish. For his part, Sibun, the classic headstrong, new kid on the block, wanted to forget the history and just go for the now of what he was trying to accomplish. Throughout the sessions, the pair had resolved their issues by holding fast in their respective attitudes.

Through it all, the resulting record would turn out to be actually pretty good. And in the end, it would leave a rather unpleasant memory to file away for future reference. Brown would realise that he did not have to say yes to everything.

One thing Brown did say yes to was a bit of a trade-off. Brown had met trumpeter Calvin Owens during the Sibun sessions and they had formed a fast friendship. As payback for helping Owens find a label to release his music in Britain, Brown was offered the opportunity to play percussion on a short tour of England.

At that point, Brown was reluctant to do gigs, not feeling his percussion skills were up to scratch. But the chance to go on the road again, even in a limited capacity, proved too great and so he said yes. Brown was enjoying the early stages of the tour, the idea of playing live in front of an audience was exhilarating. Unfortunately, Brown would have another attack of gout at some point in the tour that effected his right hand and would make playing percussion an extremely painful experience.

An experience proving uncomfortable in its own way was that with Sheridan recently taking on the role of a fulltime aerobics instructor while continuing to study acting had suddenly thrust Brown into the position of being a house father/domestic surrogate father to Sheridan's eight-year-old son Tad. It was with the best of intentions that Brown would give the job his best shot, occasionally coming close to mayhem and, at the end of the day, proving to himself and anybody who would listen that he was eminently unqualified to be around children in any way.

Brown's tour of duty as a parent had coincided with a slow period work wise. No work and too much idle time had left Brown dramatically overweight through overeating and a strong desire to get back on the road. A series of Alexis Korner memorial concerts in Germany, in which Brown would perform among the gods Jimmy Page, Robert Plant, Chris Farlowe and good friend Dick Heckstall-Smith, scratched the itch a bit, as did an invitation from back in the day when Mike Horovitz to play a bit of drums alongside some heavy jazz cats in a bit of jazz/poetry event.

Then Jack called. It was not the usual creative call to arms brought on by a new solo album but rather a BMI awards dinner in which Bruce and Brown would be honoured for the song 'Sunshine Of Your Love' having reached one million plays in America. It was ironic for Brown, still not being able to be arrested in the UK by the Brits only to receive an honour for a success in America. All Brown could do was, figuratively, throw up his hands at it all.

The remainder of 1995 would be a testament to Brown's drive and to never throwing in the towel because the last months of the year would be conspicuous by its ups and downs.

On the upside, Brown would reconnect with Dick Heckstall-Smith and The Eddie Martin Band for invigorating live shows in which Brown, front and centre on stage, would belt out the blues, and laying to rest the notion that he could not sing. The downside would be yet another attempt by Brown to find a manager to take care of his business. The former manager of guitarist Gary Moore crossed his path and the first of what would be several proposed meetings were scheduled. When the manager failed to show up at a trio of meetings, Brown took the hint and went looking elsewhere.

What had turned into an ongoing pet project, to facilitate the resurrection of the legendary Duffy Power, had finally struck paydirt. Brown had negotiated a label deal and had gone into the recording studio with a first-rate band that included Jack Bruce, Danny Thompson, Jim Mullen, Clem Clempson and Frank Tontoth. They were three-quarters of the way through recording sessions that Brown was convinced would result in an amazing album when the shit unexpectedly hit the fan. The record label had suddenly gone belly up and the liquidators swooped in and snapped up everything of value, in this case being all the tapes of the Duffy Power sessions, never to be seen or heard again.

Brown and former member of the Bonzo Dog Doo-Dah Band, Viv Stanshall had forged an unlikely relationship over the years. Respected as fellow travellers in the music world, there would be those moments when Stanshall, who had developed an often-debilitating drinking problem, would ring Brown up at all hours of the day and night in a panic. Brown would end up going to Stanshall's house and spend hours trying to talk him down from the latest round of alcohol fuelled panic attacks.

Stanshall was found dead on the morning of 6th March 1995, after an electrical fire had broken out as he slept in his top floor flat in Muswell Hill, North London.

The end of 1995 would seemingly typify where Brown's odyssey was heading. A major highlight was a live performance of the best moments of the album *Rattlesnake Guitar*. Brown's longstanding affinity for war films would also be called into play when Phil Ryan, who was undertaking a mammoth series of books on different film genres, asked Brown to do a book on war films. He was like the proverbial kid in the candy store as he set about writing a total of sixty essays on the complete history of war time movies. Brown's book would never be published.

# WHAT A DRAG

Virgin Airlines touched down in New York City. It had been a fairly comfortable flight. Flying first class usually was and one could not top the free food served to those who did not have to settle for coach. The plane came to a halt. Passengers disembarked. One passenger would need help. Pete Brown was in a wheelchair and he was in some discomfort.

1996 had started out with Brown not in too shabby a shape. He had become a bit of a political and social gadfly in the neighbourhood, becoming involved in petitions and such and flexing some long dormant liberal muscles. He was also suddenly becoming quite adept on the domestic front, enjoying the kind of father/son things with Tad. He was also becoming quite involved with his daughter Jessica who had evolved into quite the singer and Brown was now conspicuous in the audience for quite a few of his daughter's performances.

Then, right about the time, work offers were starting to trickle in once again from the United States. The first was an offer to produce an album by Swedish singer and guitarist Clas Yngström. The second, and most likely the most intriguing to Brown, was a Polygram conglomerate's decision to have him produce a Graham Bond Organisation box set. It all sounded good because, among other things, money was starting to get tight in the Brown household and any trip to the US was worth saying yes to.

As fate would have it, a monster of an attack of gout, a multi-muscle hurt with a whole lot of pain to boot, slammed Brown where it hurt the most, which seemed like everywhere. Brown tried to put off the work until the gout eased up, but he was fighting a losing battle with the pain compounded by the fact that the US jobs were threatening to go elsewhere. So he sucked up the pain, hopped on the next available flight to the states and began the jobs.

Physical pain aside, Brown would find the Yngström session fairly enjoyable, largely due to the presence of Dick Heckstall-Smith and vocalist Mary Wilson, formerly of The Supremes. A visit to a local osteopath would relieve the pain somewhat. Then it would be on to Graham Bond Organisation research, once again aided by Heckstall-Smith, that discovered a number of four track tapes that they dutifully remixed. Brown would return to the UK quite proud of the work that had been done to resurrect the Graham Bond material only to discover that Polygram was bought out by Universal whose initial work on cleaning house was to throw out the Graham Bond project.

But Brown would barely have time to lick his wounds on that rejection when a sudden resurgence in British blues and rhythm & blues, an album was put together as a bit of a tribute to the late singer and harp player Cyril Davies with Brown once again producing. For Brown, this would be a triumph of sorts when Peter Green, owing perhaps to the success of *Rattlesnake Guitar*, not only came out of retirement but also put together his own band for the purpose of playing on the album. Also chiming in to perform an appropriate song of their choosing were Jack Bruce, Clem Clempson, Georgie Fame, Maggie Bell, Brown, Phil Ryan and, contributing a great sax workout, Dick Heckstall-Smith.

The sessions could not have gone better for Brown. Green was quiet, modest and a welcome addition to sessions in which everybody seemed to get along. With one, not surprising, exception. Jack Bruce took the occasion of what had fast become a crowning achievement for Brown as producer to throw water on the event when he became noticeably unpleasant at the idea that he was being produced by Brown.

But everybody else's ego would survive in grand fashion. Including one Mick Jagger who, at the request of his brother

Chris, showed up and laid down some tasty mouth harp licks on his brother's session.

Brown and Ryan could not stand on their laurels for too long and were immediately back in the studio crafting more demos and hoping for another deal. The reality would be that it would be another decade before another label would take the bait. But Brown would remain busy, thanks in no small measure to Bruce who, on the occasion of signing a lucrative deal with German label GNP, was bound and determined to pay off the contract in record time.

Brown would turn some royalty money without having to do much with the live album *Cities Of The Heart* (1994) which featured Cream chestnuts. The traditional studio albums, *Somethin Els* (1993) and *Moonjack* (1995) would require brainstorming with Bruce. Brown recalled that during sessions for those albums, Bruce, could be as contrary and unpredictable as ever but that they nevertheless resulted in some quite good material.

By the beginning of 1997, Brown, despite his best efforts, was in deep financial difficulties. And Brown, in an anecdote from *White Rooms & Imaginary Westerns*, he acknowledged that he had no one to blame but himself. He knew he was bad in managing his money, like a lot of creative types traditionally have been. And he was decades removed when vices like alcohol and drugs had a chokehold on his wallet. The reality was that Brown's drive to be creative had often blinded him to making a decent living.

"I was in the habit of making records that didn't sell, doing gigs that didn't pay and working for dodgy and underfinanced labels. Living in a big old house, which half the time was falling apart, especially if you haven't done it before and have no idea how it was supposed to work."[140]

# I CAN DO THAT

Make no bones about it. Brown was in the dumps, at a loss of where to turn next in a career that he had willingly watched bounce up and down and often on the brink and only rarely on solid ground. But Brown, ever the realist, knew that the only way out was to find a way out. Which was to say yes to everything.

But Brown had also come to the realisation that he needed to be ready with an advanced course in getting his act together, He began with a self-imposed crash course in musical theory, with an emphasis on piano, vocals and harmony. This, he reasoned, would make him more versatile to a wider group of musicians, producers, and labels. Encouraged by his wife to become more physically fit, Brown embarked on a physical approach to his body. The gym had always been alien territory but the gym is where he went. Lifting weights was a battle won. He would also celebrate the new and improved Brown by giving up meat for good. If the opportunities presented themselves, he was determined to be road ready.

And little by little, the phone once again began to ring. Granted, writing some music for Dick Heckstall-Smith for a TV special about vegetarian anarchists fighting a legal battle with McDonalds, doing some minor production and writing work for Carmel, a band who had recently been dropped by Warner Bros and was more of a favour than a money maker and the seemingly never ending demoing between Brown and Ryan was doing little more than keeping Brown busy, that was enough for a time.

But when playing before a live audience was once again in Brown's head, he managed to snag a gig as a permanent member of The David Hadley Band as triple threat as percussion, harmonies and, as time went on, lead singer. As it stood, the David Hadley gig would be the high point of 1997 as Brown slowly but surely began to get his confidence back as somebody who could still find work and make a living.

But not surprisingly, the world of Pete Brown had fewer hits and a lot more misses when it came to gigs. In one instance, Brown was offered the opportunity to both play drums and act in a film. Brown practiced diligently and, according to onlookers, was quite up to snuff in both categories. Unfortunately, the praise was shortly followed by the budget being pulled.

The death of the film project would pre-date more runs of death and darkness, both personal and professional in the coming months. Brown would land a gig doing percussion for a true underground/eccentric legend Lady June. A former model turned poet, songwriter and recording artist for Virgin in the 1970s, she was the perfect temperamental match when, upon attempting a late in life comeback, she recruited Brown to play drums and percussions on some of her recording sessions. Brown enjoyed being around her and liked the idea of playing with a true bohemian legend, but he was also perceptive enough to realise that she was not in the best of health and would subsequently die during the recording session.

A much more emotional moment came with the news that Jack Bruce's son, Joey, died suddenly at age 29 of a severe asthma attack. Brown was distraught at his partner and friend's loss. He would recall that his reading a poem at the funeral service would bring Bruce and Brown much closer together.

Brown would often stop short of saying that his luck often seemed to be running to the dark, ironic and surreal side. The fact that his decision to go all healthy was followed by the deaths of people he knew seemed more coincidence than anything else. A case could easily be made that his erratic professional life could be the result of ignorance of the business world or a bad spat early on with the elder gods. But it seemed that, at the end of the day, his mantra for everything that had gone down in his life had been to just roll with it.

That would definitely be the case with the three gigs that ended 1997 which Brown could only describe as "bizarre". In order of appearance: Brown playing drums, dressed in a suit in front of a completely empty Italian restaurant. A Christmas gig in which, during the final song, a pile of chairs fell on the drummer, causing injury that required hospitalisation and, in the end, performing as part of a sixties revival show which toplined good buddy Arthur Brown. A bunch of musicians in the late nineties revisiting the sixties. I would say "bizarre" was the right word for it.

Going into 1998, Brown saw his growing interest from the German music and arts community result in a bit of an upswing work wise. Through his connection with Heckstall-Smith, Brown's adherence to the blues would result in his writing lyrics for an upcoming album by The Hamburg Blues Band.

Around this time, Brown also began working with what he tossed off in *White Rooms & Imaginary Westerns* as "a strange troglodyte hippie jazz/fusion composer named Wolfgang Mirbach."[141] Another obscure adventure that went nowhere in Brown's memory.

And finally, and this most certainly was the toughest assignment, reviewing a seemingly endless series of Nazi propaganda films for a compilation entitled *War Film Encyclopedia*, yet another Brown venture that would be dead on conception.

However, amidst the false starts and misfires, Brown had managed to cultivate a couple of fairly steady gigs. Brown had managed to work his way into being a permanent member of The David Hadley Band — based on both his talent and his ability to get along with Hadley's ego and the occasional lapse in business judgement which often resulted in the band playing low paying gigs that Hadley considered good exposure in the place of better paying jobs. And, like clockwork, calls from Bruce for what had become a fairly regular run of solo albums certainly did not hurt Brown's ever fluctuating bottom line.

As 1998 neared conclusion, Brown was the recipient of a busman's holiday when he was invited to New York for a new label launch party to play a bit with the likes of Peter Green, Rob Murray and others. The consensus of the assembled musicians was that the get together was a thinly veiled attempt by the label, and what was considered major financial backing, to sign Green to the label which would give the company instant credibility.

Brown and the others were more than happy to take advantage of excellent hotel accommodations, topflight room service from a menu fit for musicians who had not seen the likes of which in a while. Brown would savour the opportunity to perform with Etta James guitarist Rob Murray and to just hang out and be around Green whose status, in Brown's eyes grew the more he was around the self-effacing, slyly humorous musician.

For the moment, all seemed right in Brown's world after what had been an up and down year. But all's well would not necessarily end well as, shortly after the launch party, the financier who was funding everything, went bust, essentially ending the label, the relationships, and the reputations of a lot of people. Brown would, cryptically, acknowledge that there were a lot of bad feelings.

Brown packed his bags and returned to England. Ever the optimist, he chalked up some minor victories. He had met people, made some important contacts, played some alright music with some alright cats. And he sensed that there would be better days ahead.

# PETE BROWN'S EXCELLENT MISADVENTURES

1999. For Brown things seemed to be looking up. At least that's the way they looked on paper.

The good vibes left over from his trip to New York and meeting and getting along with Peter Green had survived the trip back across the Atlantic. As it turned out, Brown's then manager was also Green's manager and had persuaded Green and his band, The Splinter Group, that Brown was just the person to produce Green's next album, *Destiny Road*.

Brown was pleasantly surprised at the news. Then he was excited. He knew that this could be his breakthrough project as a producer and that would, most certainly, lead to bigger and better things. And the project definitely seemed to be something he could handle.

*Destiny Road* was decidedly a band situation and seemingly after several albums with the same line-up, a fairly democratic one. Green had only one songwriting credit on the album while Brown, for the first time in a long time, had none. The remainder of the twelve tracks was a mixture of originals by the band members, remakes and covers. Even the production credits would shake out between Brown and The Splinter Group. How easy could this get?

Not so easy.

Shortly before entering the recording studio, the entire Splinter Group original line-up, except for Green, quit for reasons unknown, leaving Brown and Green to quickly assemble a competent but essentially journeymen musicians to take over. Brown, as related in *White Rooms & Imaginary Westerns* found these replacement players to be less than enthusiastic about the project. "They were a disgruntled bunch of professionals who were reluctant to move outside of their comfort zone. Pete was playing well but the rest of the band seemed uncomfortable with anything mutually adventurous."[142]

It was not pleasant but there was reality to deal with and keeping a roof over the family's head. The first rehearsals and the subsequent demoing stage were a minefield, entrenched musicians constantly at odds with a producer who knew what he wanted to make the album work but wasn't getting it. Brown recalled that at one point "I was sorely tempted to walk but my own pride and the need to support my family kept me going."[143]

As did his wife Sheridan. She had been through the ups and downs before but, at this point things were looking fairly dire with creditors knocking on the door and Sheridan being forced to return to waitressing in order to bring in some money. With pressure mounting, Brown would push through in the recording which he critiqued was fairly decent but much of the finished product should have been left on the cutting room floor.

That *Destiny Road* would go on to do well in a commercial sense was of little consequence, adding insult to injury was the fact that he would receive no royalties other than his producer's wages.

But Brown, to his credit, was consistent and aggressive, he would lick his wounds from the *Destiny's Road* experience and jump right back into the pursuit of work and money. Meetings with Zombies vocalist Colin Blunstone (surely you remember the song 'Time Of The Season') and another stab at working with the band Carmel went nowhere.

A much encouraging, if nowhere near lucrative gig, once again with Wolfbang Mirbach's *Links 3*, had Brown producing, contributing lyrics and bits and pieces of music to an out there mix of rock, swing, bebop and funk with first rate musicians Kevin Coyne, Zoot Money, Clem Clempson, Mo Nazam and David Hadley. Epitaph on *Links 3*: All was right until the money ran out.

A much more rewarding enterprise, which would reunite Brown with former Van Der Graff Generator and friend Chris Smith, a rock opera called *Curly's Airships*. For Brown, it was that rare opportunity not to write, contributing vocals and percussion to the cause,

But some work and little pay was still leaving Brown in a constant state of near broke. In a desperate attempt to generate some cash, he signed on with a talent group called The Ugly Agency in hopes that his attitude, demeanour and looks would land him some movie and television roles. It was starting to be a running bit that Brown could not get arrested during his time with The Ugly Agency but the reality was that, for Brown, no work was no joke.

In an often-melancholy mood after the continued series of misadventures and just plain bad luck, Brown would return to writing poetry for the first time in a long time. It was nostalgic, by degrees therapeutic and a definite change of pace for the moment.

Doing poetry also seemed to draw interest from people from his past. Mike Horovitz would ring him out the blue and invite him to join his latest incarnation of his poetry and jazz ensemble for a series of shows in and around London. Harkening back to the time it all began would turn out to be a good bit of tonic who, despite his reading to a musical backing, would also play a bit of percussion. During a solo poetry show about that time, Brown would be an opening act for the headliner Arthur Brown who, on the night in question, was, to Brown's amusement far away from his crazy world persona and very much in a folk-rock mood.

In the meantime, Sheridan was doing her acting thing and managed to snag a role in a fairly low budget thriller called *Rage*. In a typical Pete and Sheridan scenario, a pivotal location fell out at the last possible moment and the producer asked them if they could use their home. With his wife having a considerable part in *Rage*, how could any loving husband resist.

Consequently, the home and the surrounding neighbourhood was turned into three days of total chaos with cast and crew speaking a myriad of languages, crowds milling about at all hours of the day and night and Brown's neighbours more than a bit bent out of shape as their normally quiet neighbourhood and lives were suddenly turned upside down.

By the time *Rage* finished filming, Brown had transformed from the good-natured eccentric on the block to the most annoying and undesirable. To add insult to this latest round of misadventure, at a screening of the completed film, the consensus was that *Rage* was not a very good film. And while Brown and Sheridan did get payment for the use of the house, Sheridan never got her acting fee.

Brown's ongoing relationship with Ryan continued into mid 1999 when Ryan's wife began to lose her eyesight and he was forced to curtail much of his and Brown's musical activities in order to stay close to home and care for his wife. Already recording sessions and upcoming gigs had to be cancelled.

Brown could not argue with Ryan's loyalty to his wife but there was his own personal dilemma to deal with. He was still in a state of constantly needing money, there was a trickle of gigs already in the can and he was always in need of more. Brown decided to reform The Interoceters with a whole new line-up and, by November 1999, the reconstituted Interoceters were playing live and would continue in its present configuration for some years. Ryan and his wife were constantly in Brown's thoughts, but he had to admit that it was great to have his own band again.

Brown spent the last months of 1999 in a reflective mood. The day-to-day hustle continued for a musician who had been creatively on the hunt for most of his life, going into 2000 and about to think about. But there were some moments that put him in a good place. He had reconnected with Heckstall-Smith and The Hamburg Blues Band and their shows in Hamburg, with Brown's ever improving vocals sounding confident in songs in which he took centre stage. And the response of German audiences was encouraging in more ways than one.

For the longest time, audiences would rekindle Brown's connection to the history of Cream, making the occasional requests for Brown to sing the likes of 'White Room' and 'Politician' in a concert setting. For the longest time, Brown had been reluctant to take that chance. He felt that to do so would create comparison between himself and Bruce's vocals. There was also a legitimate concern that Bruce would be critical of Brown's singing what he considered his songs.

Ultimately, Brown reasoned that Cream songs were also his songs as well and so, beginning with The Hamburg Blues Band at occasional German shows, he took the plunge and by all accounts his voice was up to the task and his interpretation of Cream, as well as Jack Bruce solo material went down quite well. Encouraged by the positive feedback, Brown began incorporating Cream songs into The Interoceters' live shows.

Brown doing Cream was righteous and legitimate. His singing of the likes of 'White Room' and 'Politician' was the icing on the cake.

# ROUGH AND TOUGH

To many in Pete and Sheridan's world, it all seemed too good to be true. And twenty years in, what few could doubt was that their relationship was easily the most stable in a music community where relationships lasting more than the length of a three minute 45 was often a figment of one's imagination. Going into 2000, Brown told the author that their relationship and their love was still growing strong.

"Sometimes she didn't like it when I was on the road or had to travel. But, over time, we had evolved to the point where she didn't have to worry about me being on the road and other women and sex. We were committed to each other and being with other people is not what we were doing."

Brown started out the year in a fairly predictable manner, doing a series of demos for a promising Latin band called Makor, sat in for a few gigs on percussion and, at the end of the day, no label deal was offered. Brown was not discouraged and moved on to a co-producing project that looked more promising, Dick Heckstall-Smith's latest album entitled *Blues And Beyond*.

The response by grade A musicians jumping at the chance to climb on board what was considered a fairly low budget production in which most participants received only session fees and Brown (who received only writer's royalties seemed, at first glance to be grade B at best. But no producer fee also included the likes of Jack Bruce and Peter Green (vocals), Clem Clempson and Mick Taylor (guitars), David Hadley (bass) and talented pros Gary Husband and Rab McCullough who, to a man, seemed more than willing to take the plunge.

Brown was swimming emotionally in clover at how smoothly *Blues And Beyond* was coming together. And the icing on this vinyl cake would be an appearance by John

Mayall. A second guest player everyone hoped would say yes was Ginger Baker the legendary drummer with the equally hair trigger temper. Brown and the rest crossed their fingers at the prospect of which Ginger they would get.

The Ginger they would get would be an absolute horror. Brown contacted Baker with the opportunity to appear on his long-time friend Heckstall-Smith's album and was angrily confronted by an example of how long he could carry a grudge.

Baker said no to the offer, based primarily on his feeling that Jack, and by association, Brown had deprived him, and to a lesser degree Eric Clapton, of large amounts of money by writing all of Cream's biggest hits with none of the royalty money going to him. Brown was shocked by Ginger's attack but had danced around this conflict with Ginger in the past, as he chronicled in *White Rooms & Imaginary Westerns*, what the real story was.

"When I first wrote with Cream, if someone had said that Ginger and Eric ought to have a share, I would of course have agreed. But no one did. And if Jack and I had not written those hits, Ginger would not have earned the enormous artist royalties and gig fees which made him a hell of a lot richer than me. Ginger has always claimed, as part of his dispute with Jack, they he had written the 5/4 intro to 'White Room' but the fact was that Jack had already written that out before Ginger ever played it."[144]

The irony was that, while nobody connected to *Blues And Beyond* made any huge amount of money, the album and all the hype surrounding the name players on the album did well enough that Heckstall-Smith was inundated with offers to play a series of big money shows with the musicians from the album. But Heckstall-Smith's inherent loyalty to The Hamburg Blues Band turned down all the offers on the grounds that it would interfere with The Hamburg Blues Band's touring schedule.

While Brown was basking in the glow of the Heckstall-

Smith album, his relationship with Sheridan was showing signs of discontent on both sides. Brown, who had long since become a stolid health nut, was finding it difficult to be around Sheridan, whose culture revolved around, partially, booze and cigarettes. For his part, Sheridan was finding it hard to live with somebody who was so obsessed with work. Through a bit of deep self-examination, it was determined that Sheridan was the victim of low self-esteem inflicted on her by her parents and Brown's issues stemmed from, quite simply, not working enough.

But the couple were so deeply committed to each other at that point that they managed to work things out. But it would be a prolonged and difficult struggle to put the pieces of their love together and, according to members of their tight circle, were on the verge of splitting up for good. It would take a last chance holiday in Tobago to save their relationship.

When on a day when the waves were high and Brown was feeling very much the professional swimmer, Sheridan would relate how she fell in love with Pete all over again when she saw him struggling to no avail with a huge wave which grabbed him up and deposited him in a heap on the beach.

If that didn't rekindle their relationship, nothing else would. It did and it did.

# MORE AND MORE OF THE SAME

In a backhanded sort of way, Brown had evolved into the consummate journeyman if you will. In certain circles, he was old-school reliable. Ring him up, offer him a job. Give him the parameters, the budget and get the hell out of his way and watch Brown do his thing. Which, over the years, had proven just about anything that captured his fancy.

And shortly after John Lee Hooker's death, Brown was presented something he could not say yes to fast enough, an all-star tribute to the late blues legend featuring topflight musicians from literally all around the world. Scheduled to produce fully half the songs on the album, Brown was immediately into research, exploring the myths, the realities and the personality of the character that went far beyond the music.

Gathering some of both the unsung and most respected musicians, who would singularly and as a group, explore the various musical moments in John Lee Hooker's life was a real joy with a line-up that included Jeff Beck, Jack Bruce, Gary Moore, Mick Taylor, Gary Brooker, Andy Fairweather Low and, certainly not least, Dick Heckstall-Smith. Every moment in the studio was one to remember and savour for Brown, with highest marks going, not too surprisingly, to Beck for the song 'Will The Circle Be Unbroken'.

The John Lee Hooker tribute album would prove a major feather in Brown's cap, cementing his reputation as a big-time producer who could get the best out of some of the biggest names. After a short break to recharge, Brown was contacted by his old agent and music publisher Gerry Bron to help repopulate a new incarnation of the quite successful Bronze record label.

Brown said yes to the offer but proceeded with caution. Bron could be a prickly, closed minded and an angry sort. But who could argue with somebody who had built Bronze Records into a considerable success with bands like Uriah Heep, Colosseum, Motörhead, Juicy Lucy and Girlschool? Any talent he brought to the table was going to be a rough sale.

Consequently, with the exception of jazz/blues pianist Paddy Milner, everybody Brown suggested quickly ran afoul of Bron's attitude, fixed ways and an almost uncanny ability to rub people the wrong way and. Of those Brown thought were way cool; many would find degrees of success with other labels.

Brown emerged only slightly the worse for wear, hanging out in places where musicians and other creative types gathered. Along the way, he made the acquaintance of a young filmmaker Mark A.J. Waters, fresh out of Boston University's College Of Creative Arts who was living the ex-pat life in London. Waters was about to make his first short film entitled *Sunny*, a surreal bit of business that required the presence of God. Things were going swimmingly for *Sunny* until midway through production when the actor playing the pivotal role of *God With No Eyes* had to quit because of a death in the family.

In a conversation with the author, Waters recounted what happened next. "I was in a pickle until the producer on the film, Miran Huq, mentioned Pete Brown as potentially being suitable for the part. Miran spoke with Pete and I faxed him a copy of the screenplay and I wrote on the cover Clapton's been called God for years. Now it's your turn. Pete read the script the next day and agreed to do it."

Albeit a bit reluctantly.

Brown had always felt he had a touch of the acting bug in him. But he would be hesitant when he found out that the part would require prosthetic makeup that would render his upper face non-existent as he would recall in *White Rooms & Imaginary Westerns*. "I am not an actor and never will be. Was this going to be some kind of ritual with some grizzly conclusion? Once we got to the set, I relaxed and played God as directed. In post-production, Waters asked Brown if he would mind doing the soundtrack for the film. Brown would respond with a compact percussion interlude."[145]

*Sunny* was screened in June 2002 in the basement of a Mexican bar. Waters recalled "I ended up speaking to Pete for the first time at length. At the time we talked about writing some screenplays together and, within a couple of days we started collaborating. The first screenplay we ended up writing together was about a Jewish circumcision ceremony."

As was often the case in Pete and Sheridan's world, they would occasionally find themselves with a bit of money. And when they did, they would go on holiday. In this case it was a quick jaunt to Hawaii and Los Angeles. They would return refreshed to the UK to find that there was a sudden flicker of interest in The Interoceters which resulted in a series of one-off live performances with the likes of David Hadley, Munch Moore and that chip off the Jack Bruce block, son Malcolm, which got Brown's live juices going.

In the meantime, the John Lee Hooker tribute album was doing quite well, and an all-star live version of the album was set for a show at the Fillmore West in San Francisco which would include Brown, Peter Green, Alvin Youngblood Hart and Narada Michael Walden. Brown considered the show a pleasurable experience rather than a chore, as was the case anytime he could find an excuse to go to the US.

Brown arrived back home to the news that The Interoceters had, thanks to the band's agent Don McKay, landed a semi-residency at a recently opened venue in Charing Cross Road. In the world of Brown shorthand, the gigs were good. Some money was regular, and he was thinking of a live album to be recorded during that run. It all sounded promising.

And then came a call from Jack Bruce for lyrics for his upcoming album *More Jack Than God*, with the extra added attraction of having his son along for musical support. Brown was, by now, an old hand at the Bruce business. He knew what to expect. There would be no surprises. So, he thought, what the hell?

Those close to the relationship between Brown and Bruce must have thought Brown was the classic case of a glutton for punishment. Well, it might have taken near forever for Brown to come to his senses and show a little backbone to accommodate Bruce which he would by the time of *More Jack Than God*, recorded primarily in Italy. The tension was beyond palpable. Bruce and his son were barely on speaking terms and, as for the expected unease between Bruce and Brown, Brown had finally had enough. He recalled in *White Rooms & Imaginary Westerns* that it had all reached critical mass.

"Nothing we did was good enough for him (Bruce). This had happened before, and I had put up with it. Now I was finding it oppressive. Being of a certain age, I had started to think about dignity and respect a lot; mainly that I felt I deserved some. Maybe it was irrational at that point, but I didn't want to be a doormat anymore."[146]

By the time *More Jack Than God* was completed, Brown had pretty much convinced himself that Jack and he would never work together again. But there was still that old devil artistic rights coming around the bend and Brown was certain that any issues concerning money owed would be the last straw. He would be right.

Not long after *More Jack Than God* was in the can, Brown received a phone call from Bruce who, as a matter of fact, suggested he give up half of his publishing rights on the album to him because he was the one who would be touring behind the record and so deserved the larger share.

Brown was gobsmacked. At that moment he had no idea what to say. He put Bruce off by telling him he had to think about it and then promptly dashed off an angry letter, telling Bruce that his suggestion was a betrayal of our relationship and the manifestation of a colossal ego.

Ego or not, Brown's letter must have struck a nerve or a pang of guilt in Bruce who came up with a more reasonable offer for the publishing rights. And given the circumstances, Brown had no choice but to agree, albeit through clenched teeth as he painfully acknowledged the circumstance. "I was broke, so I had no choice but to accept his new offer. The whole thing left a very bad taste in my mouth, and I was left with the feeling that there was no more mileage left in the relationship."[147]

# SIDEMAN FOR HIRE

There was an unwritten rule in the music world. And going into 2004, Brown had finally seemed to get it, albeit a bit late. In hindsight, Brown, way back in the beginning of his career, should have started out as a sideman and then graduated to leading groups rather than the other way around. Consequently into 2004, he was barely a blip when it came to landing a band leader role but was pulling down fairly regular work and was in demand as a band member. Had it have been the other way around; the story might have been different.

But the story was working out just fine. Just ask Saiichi Sugiyama, a successful lawyer by day, who also harboured dreams as a topflight blues guitarist. With one well received CD in 1994 under his belt and a growing reputation as somebody who could walk the walk, He had incorporated some 'heavy musical friends' into his world when he was introduced to Brown at a 2002 social get together.

"Pete came up to me and we started talking", Sugiyama recalled in a *Blues In Britain* magazine interview. "At one point he said, 'It's a shame that you're a lawyer.' And I said, 'I don't have to be'."[148]

They kept in touch and, in 2004. Brown was interested enough to play percussion and harmonies on a couple of Sugiyama's gigs. At one point Brown played on a Japanese record label Cream tribute promotional album. That disc showed the chemistry between Brown and Sugiyama which led to the in awe of Brown guitarist to go all fan boy. "I said to Pete 'Would you look at my lyrics?' Pete's said, 'Would you like me to write for you?' I said, 'Yes please, that would be wonderful.'"[149]

The result of what was, in all honesty, that rare quasi journeyman gig which provided dividends for all concerned as Brown co-wrote and produced the album *So Am I*. The period following his work on *So Am I* would be more of small potatoes, with small audiences and equally small pay with gigs with The Interoceters and Saiichi Sugiyama's band.

And while things had definitely cooled between Brown and Bruce following *More Jack Than God*, Brown had remained cordial with Jack's son Malcolm and, at one point, Brown and the younger Bruce went into the studio for what would be a label worthy album for Malcolm. Long story short, the album never got finished thanks to Malcolm suddenly developing a crisis of confidence in his ability to sing and the sudden realisation that Brown was too close to Jack and might cause a conflict. Brown was disappointed that the album never happened but his disappointment would be salved by more 'Journeyman' requests.

The opportunity to work on music with Santana and more recently Journey guitarist Neal Schon got him a trip to San Francisco and a rather challenging writing gig. Schon's approach, chords and grooves and nothing more, was a bit off kilter to Brown, who would end up writing lyrics and melodies for songs that have never been released. The opportunity to appear in a documentary about the British Beat poets resulted in a staged poetry reading and a trip to Chalk Farm and then nothing. Silence. Never happened. Next.

Then a rough emotional patch set in. Dick Heckstall-Smith, Jack Bruce, Phil Ryan, Jeff Nuttall, Ivor Cutler. On any given day, the news was that somebody in his world was sick, very sick or near death was a common dark distraction in Brown's life. Most were of his generation and age. But he was still hanging on.

Time had flown by on the personal front. His son Tad had grown, followed Brown on the musical path and was now about to go off to music college. Sheridan had all the expected emotions when her soon went off into the world.

Brown, given his ambivalence over the years when it came to the boy was suffering a bit of emotions of his own, a mixture of melancholy and sadness.

The remainder of 2004 was filled out with gigs with The Barrelhouse Blues Orchestra, Saiichi Sugiyama; the expected hoopla surrounding the release of The Interoceters live album amidst a smattering of gigs and, finally, near year's end... a first for Brown. After literally decades of his drum skills being called into question, Brown played drums on a recording session. But before those gigs went public, Brown would exercise yet another creative demon...

An extremely low budget film (£1,500) called *Really?* Producer Pete Brown. Status? Top secret until 2005. When a whole lot of people would know.

Pete Brown - *The Poet who Rocks*

# BROWN WATERS AND IN THE MEANTIME

*Really?* The film asked the question. What happens when reality and disintegration collide? Something pretty scary for certain. At least that was the summer 2004 premise, cobbled together on the sly and on the cheap by fledgling director and by this time writing partner Mark A.J. Waters and screenwriter Pete Brown.

Waters and Brown had clicked creatively and decided to make a feature length movie, starring Brown's wife Sheridan, on the cheap. To Brown's way of thinking, as he offered in *The Strange Brew,* why the hell not? "I've been a screenwriter for a long time, and I saw that various things were done or not done."[150]

How the collaboration between Brown and Waters would work out was anybody's guess. Going in, neither party knew for certain what would happen when egos of some proportion worked together. In a conversation with the author, Waters offered quite well thank you. "As Pete and I continued to write more together, it became very clear at times what we were doing at times was a kind of 'joint brain'. Sometimes that would mean that one of us could complete the other's idea with seemingly no effort at all. What I realised very quickly about Pete is that he sticks to what he believes in and doesn't care what he has to sacrifice to see his vision realised."[151]

Brown's determination was nothing new to Waters, in fact long before Brown and he had met, Brown's bravado and, yes, possible career suicide were already the stuff of legend as Waters related to this author. "In the mid-seventies the famous director Martin Scorsese had asked Pete to work with another screenwriter to create an original screenplay that

Scorsese would direct. Pete turned him down. He had decided to return to England in order to continue his music career. This would turn out to be a disaster because when he arrived back in England, he discovered that the music business had completely gone over to punk. Once we started working together, I expressed to Pete how painful I found it that he had thrown away such an amazing opportunity."[152]

But all that questionable judgement magically morphed into something seemingly more legit and sensible when, in 2005, Brown, Waters and editor Miran Huq decided to form their own production company, Brown Waters and be more professional. And by association, to have a proper, professional unveiling for the film. *Really?* had its official premiere at The Soho Hotel, well attended and received, with particular kudos to Sheridan's performance. Wasting little time, Brown and Waters quickly came up with a scenario of a noir western for the first full length feature. They would quickly discover the current status of the British film industry could be as shaky as the music business and their brainchild would go begging.

But Brown and Waters were persistent if nothing else. With no investor money in their immediate future, they plunged ahead, scouting locations, and connecting with actors for a great idea that seemed a long way from being made. Brown, who was used to juggling several balls at once, added the film business to a long list of seemingly never-ending music gigs and opportunities.

He was close to getting a go on the next Brown/Ryan record when Robert Wyatt, the singer who had been relied on to sway investors, backed out over creative issues. He would continue with sporadic gigs in the Saiichi Sugiyama band and participate in several Dick Heckstall-Smith memorial shows and an Arthur Brown retrospective show.

Aways into 2005 and the big news, only indirectly as it pertained to Brown, was the much-hyped Cream reunion show. Brown was tempted to go but when no official invite from the band was forthcoming, Brown's bad brushes with Jack Bruce and Ginger Baker over the years resurfaced and he decided to pass... Until the last minute when his filmmaking partner happened upon some tickets and gave him one. Brown accepted the ticket and, admittedly, was of two minds the night of the show. The personal grudges were still lingering in the background but, at the end of the day, he had to admit that the years had actually made them better players.

Cream mania was suddenly back in vogue and quite a few opportunists were swooping in to make something of it. One of those whose involvement, albeit minor, was Saiichi Sugiyama. Sugiyama promoted an upcoming show as featuring the guy who wrote Cream's hits as a come on.

Brown considered it a tacky and exploitive thing to do but had to admit that the show did draw an interesting and enthusiastic audience. Among those in attendance would be Brown's future manager Jon Brewer. Brewer, who once managed the likes of Yes, Mick Taylor and Alvin Lee before turning his attention to filmmaking, was shooting a Cream documentary and asked Brown to sit still for an interview. Brown agreed to do the interview, and along the way, Brewer dropped a bit of a bombshell on Brown. It seemed that the members of Cream had renegotiated their publishing deals without telling him. Brewer asked if he needed any help in sorting this potential legal mess out. He said yes and just like that Brown had another manager.

While all the music/Cream miasma was swirling around Brown's head, some actual progress was being made on Brown and Waters filmmaking venture. *Really?* had been entered in quite a few film festivals and had actually been screened at several to positive response. But when it came to the never-ending quest for budget money for their urban noir western feature, Brown recalled that if it wasn't one thing it was another.

"We had discovered that our first intended feature film was too expensive for Mark to be allowed to direct. So we picked a lower budget idea that had been lying around for a while and rewrote it. It was called *Drinking Ink*, a rite of passage dark comedy about two incompatible people."[153]

*Drinking Ink* would meander through the casting stage but there would be little or no progress beyond that point. Which left Brown more time on the music scene, which going into 2006 seemed to be picking up steam on certain fronts. Several gigs with The Hamburg Blues Band, with the occasional festival setting thrown in for good measure, began to feature Brown front and centre on a more regular basis. Brown also would return to some semblance of his sixties roots when he would back other poets on percussion during their readings. And, in a festival setting that, to Brown, was tinged in irony, when he was joined during a Hamburg Blues Band performance by Clem Clempson, Chris Farlowe and Mike Harrison for a rousing rendition of 'Sunshine Of Your Love'.

Lest anyone think that Brown's workaholic nature had once again surfaced, leaving his family home and alone, Brown, these days, was finding his family working as much as he was. In some cases, more.

Sheridan's workload was beginning to pick up. She was bagging the odd television commercial, but it would be what critics would consider an astounding performance as an elderly servant in a Strindberg play that caught the attention of critics on the little theatre beat... Equally successful was stepson Tad who joined a folk-rock band after scoring a song on the soundtrack in the American television series *Grey's Anatomy*. Brown recalled that the band ran afoul of some very familiar business shenanigans.

"Their British management managed to wreck a very

good record deal and then it was all downhill. At one point they did a thirty-gig support tour with The Proclaimers. They were sleeping in a truck and earning no money."[154]

Brown knew that it wasn't right or fair. But he could look in a mirror and know that it was all too familiar.

Pete Brown - *The Poet who Rocks*

# FRONT TO BACK TO FRONT MARRIAGE, CANCER AND OTHER THINGS

Pete and Sheridan had been together a long time. Twenty years to be exact. It had been a relationship like most others, the good, the bad, the everyday real-world things that made love and romance what it was. There was only one thing missing and, at a certain point, Sheridan was quick to cut to the chase.

"Sheridan told me that we had gone far too long without being married," Brown recalled. "We had indeed been together for twenty years and had somehow managed to stay that way, a miracle in itself considering the people involved. So we shook hands on it."[155]

The Hamburg Blues Band had evolved into Brown's bread and butter gig. He could always count on the band, especially the frequent gigs in Germany, to bring some money in. To a lesser degree, Brown could always count on The Interoceters for a live show or two but nothing approaching the kind of touring schedule that would make for a reasonable amount of money on a regular basis to live comfortably on, let alone help fill the ongoing quest for film investors.

Long story short. Brown was soon in what seemingly had become an endless hunt for an agent which resulted in father going to son for a contact. Tad's band's agent had managed to keep the band afloat despite questionable management and, in the case of Brown, seemed keen to work in some veteran musicians on her roster of youthful artists. But the agent was upfront; there was only so much that could be done unless there was a record out. Brown held out for the best and prayers were answered when singer Chris Farlowe's manager hooked up Brown and band with a series of three shows in Russia. For Brown, the brief sojourn into Russia was like entering alien turf, part musical gig, part supervised tour and finally part psychological insight into just what made Russia and its people tick. It was far from a wasted trip but, by the time the band returned to the UK, Brown had something more pressing on his mind.

Prior to going to Russia, Brown had been suffering from a nagging gum infection which his dentist tried, unsuccessfully, to cure. Thinking it might be something more serious, the dentist referred the musician to the Maxillofacial Unit at University College Hospital. Brown had always been leery of doctors and hospitals and so put off the visit until the Russia trip and, upon his return, a couple of Interoceters shows, before giving in and going to University College Hospital where they quickly cleared up the gum infection.

That was the good news.

The bad news was that during a routine biopsy as part of his treatment, doctors had discovered that Brown might have a rare form of cancer. While he was being given the bad news in detail, a surgeon joined the impromptu consultation and offered that, if Brown did, in fact, have this rare form of cancer, a cure would require a procedure in which part of his jaw would be removed and replaced with a metal plate.

Brown's response was to lapse into a complete state of denial, fear and the desire to run from the prognosis in any direction possible. Perhaps to salve his by now abject fear, the doctors immediately scheduled another biopsy and a series of scans in order to monitor the cancer. Brown was in no hurry to rush into the inevitable but decided to put it off as long as possible.

And the only way he knew how to do that was to stay busy. Which for a time consisted of near constant festival hopping, beginning with a stint at the Cannes Film Festival in which Brown, Waters and Miran did the investor hustle for their fledgling production company. The upshot was they saw the sights, met a lot of people and came away with zero financial support. Brown would go solo with shows, in West Hampstead and, along with The Barrelhouse Band, in Dorset.

Then, with the insistence that it was time to make it all legal, and with the spectre of cancer concerns ever present, Pete and Sheridan decided to tie the knot. It would be a fairly simple in and out ceremony at the local registry office. Heartfelt speeches and an emotionally charged selection of songs accompanied the ceremony as selected by Brown, 'First Time Ever I Saw Your Face' and 'Motion'. Then it was back home for some emotional, musically charged moments by musician friends. A week later, Pete and Sheridan on their honeymoon, spent much of being newly married enjoying life, love and bickering a bit. At the end of the stay, life and love won out.

Honeymoon concluded, life returned to normal which, for Brown, meant another gig in *Dorset*, playing Interoceters songs. This followed by an immediate, marathon recording session of new Interoceters/Phil Ryan songs. The cancer tests were showing that Brown should definitely be going to have the operation sooner rather than later and that he was feeling an urgency to get something new and Ryan centric down for posterity. As he recalled in *White Rooms & Imaginary Westerns*, his legacy and mortality were very much in play.

"I can't deny that I did those sessions because I wasn't sure that I would survive long enough to do the record with Phil. I wanted there to be a studio recording of The Interoceters and also some representation of how I was singing, which was a lot better than before."[156]

With those sessions out of the way, Brown seemed suddenly even more apprehensive when the doctors gave

Brown a 25th September 2006 date for his operation. And more intent on doing it all while he felt he could. A poetry and song appearance in a favourite stomping ground, West Hampstead segued into a trip for an appearance at a Peace Festival in Galway after which he guested at the Cologne Blues Festival with the Hamburg Blues Band.

All of which led up to September, which would kick off in dark style. Ryan's long-suffering wife had passed, and Pete and Sheridan went to the funeral. If it were a bad omen for Brown's impending operation, he would not say. But on 25th September, it was a safe bet that it was on his mind.

The surgeon heading up the procedure was well aware of Brown's fear of losing his voice and, in a sense, his life. He was sympathetic and had come up with a compromise to the operation. Rather than an extreme removal of jaw tissue and inserting a metal plate, he would only cut away the affected gum tissue.

Nevertheless, it would be an arduous ordeal. It would be the first time that Brown had ever spent the night in a hospital and he shuddered at the prospect of a sleepless night. That was remedied by a powerful medication that kept him under for the duration of the operation. When he came out of it, Brown's voice was noticeably lower. Not surprisingly, he was not at his best after the procedure.

But after a bit of rest and recovery, Brown happily discovered that he could still sing. To celebrate, he immediately got back to work on a truly three ring creative circus at the rejuvenated Marquee Club in which Brown would recruit the likes of Arthur Brown, David Amram, Michael Horovitz, Brown and a revolving assortment of musicians and poets and the result was a mixture of old and new performing styles. The new Marquee Club would ultimately have a short shelf life and would be the gig where The Interoceters would finally pack it in. But this would not be the last moments in Brown's post operative busy work.

A phone call from the states would send Brown back to the US to help a musician with producing aspirations with lyrics and arrangements. His stamina would be further tested when he received a call to appear at a Rory Gallagher tribute show. It was at that point that Brown started to not feel right and, when the producing gig fell through and he had to endure a hellish flight home, he could tell, as he recalled in *White Rooms & Imaginary Westerns*, that 'not feeling right' had morphed into something a bit more concerning.

"After the operation, all of this must have been too much too soon. I should have been taking it easier. But I didn't. On the flight home, I was finding it difficult to sleep. When I got back to Heathrow, I didn't feel great and by the time I got home I was feeling worse. I went to a local hospital where they did some tests and found nothing. So, I went home."[157]

Except a nagging uncertainty about the future and, once again the notion of writing his autobiography. Brown had a connection with an author named Harry Shapiro (no relation) who was quite well versed in the life and times of Brown. Having done a well-received biography on Jack Bruce Shapiro began a bit of research that would result in a couple of sample chapters that would be submitted to Brown's friend and publisher Jeremy Robson of JR Books who was increasingly interested in doing the book. Brown recalled that there would be one caveat.

"At that point, I was hoping that somebody else would write the book. But Jeremy decided that my story should be told in my voice. I was now about to be my own autobiographer."[158]

Pete Brown - *The Poet who Rocks*

# THE RELUCTANT BIOGRAPHER

Nobody can argue with the fact that Pete Brown has led a life worth writing about. But in lesser hands, that fine line between the subject and the author of the book can be a slippery slope. Witness for the defence is Pete Brown. Subject of this book is *White Rooms & Imaginary Westerns: On The Road With Ginsburg, Writing For Clapton And Cream, Anarchic Odyssey*. Brown's autobiography was published in 2010.

Here's Pete for the defence, in a Cherry Red TV interview, as to why his book reads the way it does. "I'm a collaborator. In all my writing endeavours, I would like to work with other people. I really need a lot of people to work off of because I am a social animal."[159]

Which why, when it was determined that Pete would have to write his book in his voice, he did an emotional double take for the Cherry Red TV interviewer. "The hardest thing I had to do when the deal for the book was struck was to write my own autobiography. It was hellish. Two and a half years of sitting at the computer by myself. It really hurt a lot. Not that I wasn't capable of writing the book myself. It's just not me. And, at times, it was very painful."[160]

But in the book's defence, *White Rooms & Imaginary Westerns* is far from a predictable series of pop culture anecdotes we, with slight variations, have read before in other biographies. Brown was well aware of his place in the universe and was not going to shy away from it. "I was trying to be different," he explained to Cherry Red TV. "I was trying to be honest. I am a mad artist. So I wanted it to be about failure and frustration and just the way things were. I wanted it to not just be about bullshit."[161]

"I am not a book writer," he quipped to *Quavoid World*

*Press*. "That gave me a signal about how I would write my book. I was not going to try and write beautiful writing. I was going to write it how I would speak it."[162]

# SMILE FOR THE CAMERA

A bit of tie in never hurt. Especially when it came to *White Rooms & Imaginary Westerns: On The Road With Ginsberg, Writing For Clapton And Cream: An Anarchic Odyssey*. The book arrived in 2010 with a whole lot of hype and a modicum of interest. An honest assessment was that reviews were mixed. Some loved Brown's style of writing. It was like one was in the room with him as he was telling his stories. Some had a bone or two to pick. A bit too much of 'and then I did this and such'. But nobody could argue with the fact that Brown was being an honest chronicler of his life and times.

A tie in documentary about Pete, narrated by Pete and featuring interviews with all manner of names in his personal and professional life was directed by his partner in film adventures Mark A.J. Waters. All wrapped up in a somewhat mystical vibe in keeping with Pete's personality, this was a damned good idea as well.

The fact that Brown and Waters had already had a handful of earlier film projects shot down by investors did not dissuade them. They were convinced that a *White Rooms & Imaginary Westerns* documentary would work. Brown and Waters had long been in synch, knowing their respective quirks and idiosyncrasies in fine detail. But putting Brown front and centre, well that had the intention of getting quite personal was a whole different notion that would need to be hashed out.

Owing to the often-leisurely nature of the documentary process, *White Rooms & Imaginary Westerns* would take its time getting off and running. The plan was for the film to begin actual shooting in 2011 but, given the often roller coaster nature of the business, the real intense nature of the filmmaking process would take place between 2013 and 2016.

The blueprint would be a guided tour of Brown's life, the social, political and, by degrees, the impressionistic, in a tone in keeping with Brown's attitudes and philosophy. They would both agree that the personal, the enlightening, the entertaining and humane was the Pete Brown that should go in front of the camera. People who knew Brown from various moments in his life, wife Sheridan, from the poetry days Michael Horovitz and musicians David Amram, George Kahn, Robert Wyatt, Jon Hiseman, Phil Ryan, Chris Spedding et al, were more than willing to sit for the camera.

But what about the members of Cream? Had too many bridges been burned with Brown and, for that matter, Bruce to sit the former power trio down for a real, penetrating series of no holds barred candour?

Eric Clapton had less of any real or imagined beef with Brown. With Jack Bruce and Ginger Baker, things had gotten dicey over the years on a number of issues. Would the pivotal members of the group be inclined to step to the plate and cooperate? Once filming begun and proceeded over an extended number of years in fits and starts, Brown and Waters would have their answer as typified by a Waters Facebook entry in 2015.

"We interviewed Eric Clapton this afternoon, a very cool interview, a very cool human being. Now we have Martin Scorsese, Jack Bruce, Ginger Baker and a whole lot of other fascinating people to tell Pete's story."[163]

But the documentary ride would be a bit bumpy as Waters would remember in an interview with the author. "All the guys in Cream were super nice. They all welcomed us into their homes to talk about Pete. The Baker family invited us in and treated us to an afternoon tea while we set up to interview Ginger. Jack was very insightful, and his humour was much in evidence. Eric was a charming host. What the bandmembers had to say about each other, particularly Jack and Ginger, was, at times, less than complimentary. I've included all of those bits in the film."

For his part, the director found Brown the ideal subject as well as somebody who moved easily through the often-hectic process. "Pete was cooperative. He never vetoed anything that I did or any sequences that I did. He put up with flack being thrown at him, in particular by Ginger, no matter how uncomfortable he felt about it."

To what degree *White Rooms & Imaginary Westerns* was completed or, for that matter, even partially edited by 2014 was debatable. What is known is that by 2015 teaser clips and a short trailer began to appear on various Internet sites that looked pretty decent. From that point on, there would be the occasional bit of film biz jargon such as to be announced, deal pending or, by 2017, that ever-present kiss of death, nearing distribution deal.

Close but still no cigar. At least not yet.

"We've had several offers to distribute the film," insisted Waters. "We are almost there with a release."

# BROWN LOOKS BACK

When Brown turns reflective, he often turns to the lyrics of the classic bluesmen. And when 2010 rolled around, awash in health issues, the publication of his autobiography, life issues, family issues and a seemingly never-ending race to make something of his god given talents, one person came to mind in *White Rooms & Imaginary Westerns*. "As Screamin' Jay Hawkins once put it, 'I don't care if you don't want me. I'm yours.'"[164]

Brown and Waters kicked off the year in their endless pursuit of money to make their movie, which included a second round at the Cannes Film Festival, meeting a lot of people and still striking out when it came to the bottom line. For her part, Sheridan was continuing to pursue the actor's dream in a fringe bit of business about Jane Austin that would leave audiences underwhelmed except for Sheridan's professionalism.

Brown was not sitting idly by. He signed on for an all-star gig which featured The Hamburg Blues Band and special guests Chris Farlowe and Maggie Bell. And with return from the spiritual and emotional wilderness of Phil Ryan, the long-time friends and musical compatriots began reworking and polishing songs from their archives for the long-projected Brown/Ryan album whose final mix required a trip back to Los Angeles, for a joyous round of work, hobnobbing with celebrities and, yes, laying about by the pool. Brown was in good spirits. Everything was working like clockwork.

Until the last day in Los Angeles when Brown woke up not feeling well. Brown had been through enough of these health issues to know what came next. A trip to nearby Cedars Sinai Hospital and a battery of tests concluded with the pronouncement that he had definitely suffered some kind of heart damage, with a bypass operation a clear option according to the doctors. One doctor went so far as to predict if Brown had gone ahead with plans to fly home the next day, there was a good possibility that he might have a heart attack in flight.

The doctors would later modify their assessment to conclude that Brown had, in fact, suffered a somewhat less critical blocked artery which would be corrected with a forty-five-minute procedure called a 'routine angioplasty'. A week of post operative recovery time and a non-eventful flight back to England where Sheridan and Tad waited to give Brown the right amount of TLC.

Brown was suddenly thoughtful behind this latest health scare. Exercising had suddenly become uppermost, and it was something he began to take quite seriously. At the first signs of feeling a bit uneasy one session into his return to the recording studio, it was an immediate call to the doctor. He was constantly being monitored and any damage done with the blocked artery had been minimal. Brown was on top of things physically but, psychologically, there would be one more hurdle.

There was a festival appearance in Switzerland and, after already cancelling three gigs because of the illness, Brown remained reluctant to do this one but when his doctor felt it would be good to do it and so, with the fear of a heart attack still buried in his post operative psyche, he stepped on the plane headed for Switzerland.

"I felt quite nervous sitting on the plane and was tentative and not very energetic when I arrived for rehearsal with the Swiss backing band," as he chronicled in *White Rooms & Imaginary Westerns*. The next day, after the sound check, I felt happier after a good night's sleep. By the time it came time for my set, I felt more confident and the audience let me know that I was welcome."[165]

Patience and persistence would be the end game for his

long in the works Ryan/Brown opus *Road Of Cobras* that would be completed in 2009. And that rarity for Brown, a proper record deal was completed that same year. Brown would turn sixty-nine about the time *Road Of Cobras* was released. 2010 had been that kind of year.

And Brown had lived to tell about it.

## PETE MEETS PROCOL

Make no mistake. A big reason why Pete Brown has never been a well-known entity in the United States is commercial hits or the lack of same. Don't get Pete wrong. He has always wanted hits, to hear his music on the radio 24/7, and to get the notoriety, not to mention royalties and other perks that go along with commercial success. The lone exception is obviously his tenure as Cream's go to lyricist where, even in the states he has been little more than a footnote, an 'oh he wrote those songs'?

But when it comes to breakout mammoth hits outside a handful of enclaves in Europe, it has largely escaped him and that is not completely his doing.

Brown has always had a huge upside when it came to creative/commercial instincts. He's known what goes into making a commercial radio hit. But he's also been sidetracked by a simple equation, to do the music he likes. The way he likes it often ran contrary, the formula, everything that has rubbed Pete the wrong way and that he refused to go along with the program that those instincts often floundered on the reef of bad business deals, questionable marketing and management and, as they say in the bad luck bars where mishaps were always on tap, shit happens.

Brown is the closest thing to ticked off when it has been suggested that he is up for anything if there's a cheque at the end of it. As witness the time *Louderthansound.com* suggested as much. "I'm not really a songwriter for hire. That's not my thing. I will get involved with projects that interest me creatively or musically. That's what I do."[166]

To be sure, Brown has been bitten by any and all bad luck. But, in all fairness, he has had his share of reasonably well-known acts that have sold a considerable number of albums to be considered hits of a kind.

Cream. Enough said. Jack Bruce. Solo. A bit inconsistent but always in the ballpark when it came to Bruce's music finding an audience. West, Bruce & Laing. I know. I'll get an argument out of this one. But West, Bruce & Laing got a bit of the pie during their short reign and Brown got his share of the bit. Nothing to write home about but a taste is still a taste if it has your name written on it.

And let's be honest, by the mid-2000s, bands and musicians with some semblance of a career, a hit or two have sought Pete out to work that self-same commercial magic on a rep that, to many observers, might have gone a little tepid and stagnant.

In 2017, Procol Harum came calling.

Procol Harum, a mixture of highbrow prog rock since the mid-sixties, have been marked by often maddening inconsistences and rock and roll drama while creating one major hit in 'A Whiter Shade Of Pale', a close runner up in 'Conquistador' and 'So Rightly So' and a balls out rocker, most likely just to prove they could do one, in 'Whisky Train'. But the band would spend a good chunk of their existence mired in line-up changes, prolonged hiatus, lawsuits, band member beefs and creative differences. When Pete got the call, Procol Harum were attempting their first album of new music in 14 years.

Pete remembered in *Louderthansound.com* seeing Procol Harum in places like London's UFO Club as far back as 1967. "Years later, when they were thinking about recording *Novum*, they thought about me doing it. It was coming up on an anniversary of sorts and Gary Brooker, also in *Louderthansound.com* put the decision this way. "We'd been going like this for fifty years. It was time for us to make some effort."[167]

The meeting between Brooker and Brown was brief as

Brown recalled in *Louderthansound.com*. "I asked Gary if he had any idea for the theme for the album? He said 'Yeah. The Ten Commandments.' I said okay even though I was nowhere as religious as Gary was. We drifted away from that idea but there would be some elements inspired by it. As it would turn out, the album would turn out not so much to be about God as it was about a slimy rock and roll manager."[168]

*Novum* would carry all the hallmarks of Brown's skills. He would contribute lyrics to nine of the eleven songs on the album and each song would contain more thought provoking and real world attitudes and, yes, no small amount of Brown's sense of humour.

Pete Brown - *The Poet who Rocks*

# THIS YEAR LOOKS GOOD ON PAPER

If you're a diehard Pete Brown completist, take note. Somewhere in some musty, dusty used vinyl bin is a very hard to find old Battered Ornaments single entitled 'This Year Looks Good On Paper'. It's a clever bit of irony, very Pete like and, in execution, very telling. Going into 2019, Brown may well have had that song on his mind.

On the occasion of turning eighty, Brown was, in short order, the recipient of a trio of major health issues, to wit a heart bypass operation, a bleeding ulcer and a successful small cancer operation. Away from the operating table, Brown's professional luck did not run any better as the long anticipated *White Rooms & Imaginary Westerns* documentary continued to search for a distribution deal to no avail.

But ever the fighter, Brown took the occasion of this run of bad luck, which was to brush past the harsh times and hustle up another gig ... or several. First out of the blocks, and sentimental in nature would be the last album between Brown and Ryan, entitled *Words Of Wisdom* and his backing band Psoulchedelia. The album, thematically, was old school and inspirational, especially with the songs 'Don't Want Anything Old In My Life' and 'Go Down Fighting'

True to the song's sentiments, Brown, always up for the challenge despite assorted drawbacks, remained busy during the year. The fact that Brown continued to be a fairly low-key presence in the US, there was talk of serious American tour dates in the coming year. One thing for certain, more and more musicians were beginning to get hip to Brown's thing and he would end up contributing lyrics to such US musicians as Joe Bonamassa and Carla Olson. There was also a handful of gigs in London and Norway with recent protégé Krissy Matthews. And 2019 would see two years in the making all-star collection entitled Cream Acoustic as Brown offered in *All About Jazz.com*

"It's Cream and Cream related songs done acoustically and features the last performance of Ginger Baker and contributions by Joe Bonamassa, Deborah Bonham, Maggie Bell, Malcolm Bruce and Paul Rodgers."[169]

Brown would see out 2019 on Christmas day, turning eighty, still spry and in the tradition of yet another old song, the title track from the album *Things May Come And Things May Go But The Art School Dance Goes On Forever*.

A sure reminder that for Brown the art school is still moving down the tracks.

# THE FUTURE IS IN THE MAIL

5th February 2023. This manuscript for Pete Brown: The Poet Who Rocks is due 28th February. I knew that. But just to make sure I put two and two together.

I went to Amazon and took a gander. Right next to a roaring, snarling closeup of Pete doing his thing on the cover was the on-sale date of 5th May 2023. If the publisher said it was so then I guess it was so. It was out there. The world knew it was coming. I knew it was coming. Last minute, nips, tucks, style issues and edits aside, this puppy was done. Or was it?

Brown has had his share of health issues. The 200 Fingers exhaustion episode we've already talked about. More recent episodes include his first cancer operation in 2006, one of several he's dealt with over the years. Heart bypass surgery in 2019 made him a new man. A minor stroke this year gave evidence that yes Pete Brown is eighty-two as this book is being written and... well stuff happens. But that didn't stop Brown, who has always had a touch of gallows humour to acknowledge in an email:

*"Doing a new album that is scheduled to come out in March. So I'm trying very hard to stay alive until then."*

During one of our final conversations, Brown warned me. He was going under the knife on 14th February 2023 as the result of an off and on bout with cancer in recent years. But he agreed we would talk again post operation for a first-hand report on how the operation went, how he was feeling and what the future might bring. In our final conversation before the procedure, Brown remained upbeat and hesitant about things.

*"Going through my next cancer operation, I'm not sure how much live work I'll be doing. Touring and performing can be very taxing. The touring I had been doing before*

*Christmas had been great and then I got the flu and all of a sudden I had to look at all of this again. My guess is we've got to cut back on this kind of stuff. Part of me thinks I'm getting too old for this. We'll see how I come out of this latest operation. Hopefully they'll catch it. I guess we'll just have to see how it goes."*

23rd February 2023. Received an email message from Pete: *"Dear Marc. Now out of hospital and convalescing. Having a quiet few days. It was a long operation, six hours. Couldn't speak for a week. I should be up for a phone call next week. Let me know. All The Best Pete."*

8th March 2023. Received a second post op update from Pete: *"Sorry to not have been in touch. After my big cancer operation, I had a nasty infection and had to return to the hospital for another few days. I'm just beginning to get over it. Good news. Before the operation, I did all the vocals for the record and will go into the studio on Monday for a week to record the band, horns and backing vocals. If you want to talk a bit more, then call me tomorrow (Thursday) at the usual time. Then Monday if I'm okay. After that I'm trying to get fit and ready for six weeks of bloody radiotherapy. I should be around most of the weekend. It looks like the new album will be called* Brothers And Systems. *Meanwhile all the best Pete."*

10th March 2023. Received a third post op update from Pete: *"Dear Marc. When do you think the book will actually come out?* Brothers And Systems *will be out in September. The album features Clapton, Bonamassa, Bobby Rush, Arthur Brown and Bernie Marsden. Planning on doing a lot of promotion, including some life stuff if I can cut it. I will be around this weekend and tonight if you need final details. All The Best Pete."*

And in the end. Leave it to a fellow musician/lyricist/band Timbuk 3 to succinctly nail what Brown has carried along with him for seemingly forever and will continue on as long as Pete Brown carries the spark, the drive and the will to keep doing what he's doing.

The future's so bright I Gotta Wear Shades.

Pete Brown says amen to that.

# SOURCES

All interview quotes from Pete Brown were conducted with the author except those detailed below.

1. The Argonist.com interview with Pete Brown.
2. Please Kill Me Magazine.com. Interview by John Kruth.
3. UYC Experience podcast. Pete Brown interview.
4. Historical archives covering World War II, The Blitz and the town where Pete Brown was born.
5. White Rooms & Imaginary Westerns On The Road With Ginsberg, Writing For Clapton And Cream, An Anarchic Odyssey by Pete Brown, (2010 JR Books). Excerpt.
6. White Rooms & Imaginary Westerns. Book excerpt.
7. White Rooms & Imaginary Westerns. Book excerpt.
8. White Rooms & Imaginary Westerns. Book excerpt.
9. White Rooms & Imaginary Westerns. Book excerpt.
10. Strange Brew.com. Pete Brown interview.
11. Please Kill Me Magazine.com. Pete Brown interview.
12. All About Jazz.com and White Rooms & Imaginary Westerns.
13. White Rooms & Imaginary Westerns. Book excerpt.
14. Elaine Grazen interview with author Marc Shapiro.
15. Elaine Grazen interview with author Marc Shapiro.
16. The Head And The Heart.com. Pete Brown interview.
17. White Rooms & Imaginary Westerns. Book excerpt.
18. White Rooms & Imaginary Westerns. Book excerpt.
    Poetry samples from early magazine publications.
19. Music From The Head And The Heart.com. Pete Brown interview.
20. White Rooms & Imaginary Westerns. Book excerpt.
21. All About Jazz.com. Pete Brown information and insights.
22. John Mumford interview with author Marc Shapiro.
23. Music Guy 247.com. Pete Brown interview.
24. Encyclopedia.com. Beat and Pete Brown citations.
25. All About Jazz.com
26. White Rooms & Imaginary Westerns. Book excerpt.
27. John Mumford interview with author Marc Shapiro.
28. Please Kill Me Magazine.com. Pete Brown interview.
29. Lux.org.uk.
30. Music From The Head And The Heart.com
31. Music Guy 247.com.
32. Beat Scene Magazine.
33. John Mumford interview with author Marc Shapiro.
34. All About Jazz.com.
35. Poetry Foundation.com.
36. Emptymirrorbooks.com.
37. All About Jazz.com.
38. White Rooms & Imaginary Westerns. Book excerpt.
39. The Incubator.com.
40. White Rooms & Imaginary Westerns. Book excerpt.
41. All About Jazz.com.
42. White Rooms & Imaginary Westerns. Book excerpt.
43. Please Kill Me.com, Music For The Head And Heart.com, Cherry Red TV.com.
44. Cherry Red TV.com.
45. Cherry Red TV.com.
46. Ginger Baker: Hellraiser by Ginger Baker. Book excerpt.
47. Clapton by Eric Clapton. Book excerpt.
48. Guitarist Presents: The Blues Magazine.
49. Guitarist Presents: The Blues Magazine.
50. Clapton by Eric Clapton. Book excerpt.
51. Clapton by Ray Coleman. Book excerpt.
52. Guitarist Presents: The Blues Magazine.

53. Disraeli Gears Cream by Cream (DVD).
54. All About Jazz.com.
55. White Rooms & Imaginary Westerns. Book excerpt.
56. Songfacts.com. Pete Brown interview.
57. Reason To Rock.com.
58. Songfacts.com
59. Please Kill Me.com
60. Ginger Baker: Hellraiser by Ginger Baker. Book excerpt.
61. Please Kill Me.com
62. Songfacts.com.
63. Music For The Head And Heart.com.
64. White Rooms & Imaginary Westerns. Book excerpt.
65. Chris Spedding interview with author Marc Shapiro.
66. Strange Brew.com, Music Guy 247.com.
67. Chris Spedding interview with author Marc Shapiro.
68. White Rooms & Imaginary Westerns. Book excerpt.
69. All About Jazz.com.
70. White Rooms & Imaginary Westerns. Book Excerpt.
71. Chris Spedding interview by author Marc Shapiro.
72. Chris Spedding interview by author Marc Shapiro.
73. All About Jazz.com
74. Chris Spedding interview with author Marc Shapiro.
75. Chris Spedding interview with author Marc Shapiro.
76. White Rooms & Imaginary Westerns. Book excerpt.
77. Brave Words.com.
78. Stephen Leigh.com.UK.
79. Stephen Leigh.com.UK.
80. Stephen Leigh.com.UK.
81. Strange Brew.com.
82. Ultimate Classic Rock.com.
83. Goldmine.com.
84. White Rooms & Imaginary Westerns. Book excerpts.
85. All About Jazz.com
86. Strange Brew.com
87. All About Jazz.com.
88. White Rooms & Imaginary Westerns. Book excerpts.
89. Songfacts.com.
90. White Rooms & Imaginary Westerns. Book excerpts.
91. White Rooms & Imaginary Westerns. Book excerpts.
92. Strange Brew.com.
93. White Rooms & Imaginary Westerns. Book excerpts.
94. White Rooms & Imaginary Westerns. Book excerpts.
95. White Rooms & Imaginary Westerns. Book excerpts.
96. Music For The Head And The Heart.com.
97. Record Collector.com.
98. The Generalist.com, All About Jazz.com.
99. All About Jazz.com.
100. Classic Rock Review.com
101. His Voice.com.
102. London Observer newspaper.
103. Classic Rock Magazine.com.
104. Classic Rock Magazine.com.
105. White Rooms & Imaginary Westerns. Book excerpts.
106. Strange Brew.com.
107. White Rooms & Imaginary Westerns. Book excerpts.
108. Strange Brew.com, Record Collector.com.
109. Strange Brew.com, Record Collector.com., White Rooms & Imaginary Westerns. Book excerpts.
110. White Rooms & Imaginary Westerns. Book excerpts.
111. Pete Brown Facebook entry.

112. Pete Brown Facebook entry.
113. White Rooms & Imaginary Westerns. Book excerpt.
114. White Rooms & Imaginary Westerns. Book excerpts.
115. White Rooms & Imaginary Westerns. Book excerpts.
116. White Rooms & Imaginary Westerns. Book excerpts.
117. White Rooms & Imaginary Westerns. Book excerpts.
118. White Rooms & Imaginary Westerns. Book excerpts.
119. White Rooms & Imaginary Westerns. Book excerpts.
120. White Rooms & Imaginary Westerns. Book excerpts.
121. White Rooms & Imaginary Westerns. Book excerpts.
122. Music From The Head And The Heart.com.
123. All About Jazz.com.
124. All About Jazz.com.
125. White Rooms & Imaginary Westerns. Book excerpts.
126. White Rooms & Imaginary Westerns. Book excerpts.
127. White Rooms & Imaginary Westerns. Book excerpts.
128. White Rooms & Imaginary Westerns. Book excerpts.
129. White Rooms & Imaginary Westerns. Book excerpts.
130. Strange Brew.com.
131. Strange Brew.com.
132. Strange Brew.com.
133. White Rooms & Imaginary Westerns. Book excerpts.
134. White Rooms & Imaginary Westerns. Book excerpts.
135. White Rooms & Imaginary Westerns. Book excerpts.
136. White Rooms & Imaginary Westerns. Book excerpts.
137. White Rooms & Imaginary Westerns. Book excerpts.
138. White Rooms & Imaginary Westerns. Book excerpts.
139. White Rooms & Imaginary Westerns. Book excerpts.
140. White Rooms & Imaginary Westerns. Book excerpts.
141. White Rooms & Imaginary Westerns. Book excerpts.
142. White Rooms & Imaginary Westerns. Book excerpts.
143. White Rooms & Imaginary Westerns. Book excerpts.
144. White Rooms & Imaginary Westerns. Book excerpts.
145. White Rooms & Imaginary Westerns. Book excerpts.
146. White Rooms & Imaginary Westerns. Book excerpts.
147. White Rooms & Imaginary Westerns. Book excerpts.
148. Blues In Britain magazine.
149. Blues in Britain magazine.
150. Strange Brew.com.
151. Mark Waters interview with author Marc Shapiro.
152. Mark Waters interview with author Marc Shapiro.
153. White Rooms & Imaginary Westerns. Book excerpts.
154. White Rooms & Imaginary Westerns. Book excerpts.
155. White Rooms & Imaginary Westerns. Book excerpts.
156. White Rooms & Imaginary Westerns. Book excerpts.
157. White Rooms & Imaginary Westerns. Book excerpts.
158. White Rooms & Imaginary Westerns. Book excerpts.
159. Cherry Red TV.com.
160. Cherry Red TV.com.
161. Cherry Red TV.com.
162. Qavoid World Press.com.
163. Facebook entry.
164. White Rooms & Imaginary Westerns. Book excerpts.
165. White Rooms & Imaginary Westerns. Book excerpts.
166. Louderthansound.com.
167. Louderthansound.com.
168. Louderthansound.com.
169. All About Jazz.com.

# ABOUT THE AUTHOR

Marc Shapiro is the New York Times bestselling author of *J.K. Rowling: The Wizard behind Harry Potter*, *Justin Bieber: The Fever!* and many other bestselling celebrity biographies. He has been a freelance entertainment journalist for more than twenty-five years, covering film, television and music for a number of national and international newspapers and magazines.

authormarcshapiro@yahoo.com